The Woman with the German Accent

Leaving Home to Find Happiness

Anita Gertrude Roesch Plutte

For Dawn
and family!
Love your life!
Fondly,
Anita Plutte

xulon
PRESS

The Woman with the German Accent
Leaving Home to Find Happiness
by Anita Gertrude Roesch Plutte

Printed in the United States of America

ISBN 9781619044098

www.xulonpress.com

by Anita Gertrude Roesch Plutte

I dedicate this book to the memory of my sister Renate, whose strength was enough for both of us on the day I illegally escaped from East Germany. In spite of living most of our lives physically separated, our love and support for each other never waned.

Table of Contents

Preface

—*by Janet Uetz*

Our mother (Anita Gertrude Roesch Plutte) is an ordinary person living unnoticed by those outside of her large circle of family and friends. To see the love and joy radiating from her as she enjoys life in the Pennsylvania retirement community where she lives, one would never imagine the extraordinary life journey that she has traveled. Nearing age 80, she is full of joy and vitality; she can't wait for the next bus trip; she loves to learn; she embraces the arts; she plays to win; she cherishes her friendships and her family; and she passionately gives a piece of herself to everyone she meets. People are drawn to her; they quickly become engrossed as she tells colorful stories from her life experience. She is a captivating person that you will not easily forget once you have encountered her.

Her earliest memories are of growing up in Germany during WWII. This dark period of Germany's history is well known. Our mother saw how her adult neighbors and teachers were mesmerized by Hitler's charisma almost to the point of worship. During her early years, she experienced the intense fear of frequent bomb threats that ultimately resulted in the destruction of her home. The manipulation and pressure to conform to the expectations of a Hitler Youth, left a deep wound whose scars remain. Hitler's Third Reich was set on annihilation of the Jews and domination of all of its surrounding countries. She and her family were German, not Jewish. While they did not suffer to the same horrific extent that the Jewish population did at the hands of the Nazi government during WWII, the war still wrought havoc on the German people of any religion who lived through the terror and were left to rebuild their country after the devastation of war. When Germany lost the war and the world defeated Hitler, the country was divided into two sections. West Germany was supported by the US and other democratic countries to rebuild its infrastructure. East Germany was under the governance of Russian Communism; it was largely left destroyed with no reconstruction support and no sympathy from the nations on the world stage. Our mother's family was located in East Germany. Following the brief jubilation that the war was over, life rapidly turned to the realization that they lost almost everything they had and they were facing poverty and starvation every day. Furthermore, their homeland was being set up under a communist government. To our mother, it had that same feel of fanaticism and manipulation that existed under Hitler and she was terrified of where it might lead.

By this time, she was a young adult, had dreams for her life and was anxious to build a beautiful future. However, she felt continued hopelessness in the world around her. Something within her would not settle for that. Our father, Heinz, was her boyfriend; he left East Germany a few years earlier to pursue his dream of a better life. She chose to illegally leave her home and family to follow Heinz and to begin a new life in America. She thought that she would be safe and that all her dreams for a happy marriage and a family of her own would come true in America. It was this hope that compelled her forward into the unknown.

What she didn't know is that while she would experience many moments of great joy, there would also be loneliness, heartache from a disappointing marriage, prejudice, and finally utter despair. Her story is one of seeking, yearning and giving her all to finding meaning and purpose in life despite the many hardships she faced in every season. Our mother wanted to write her life story to share what she learned; that it is not one's life circumstances that will determine one's happiness. She spent half of her life hoping that a change in where she lived, what she did or who she was with would bring her the joy and peace she was longing for. Despite her best efforts, she could not find happiness. When she finally came to the end of her own strength and was in a corner with nowhere to turn, she cried out for help to the Creator of the Universe whom she had largely ignored for most of her life. He came and answered her plea. Following that, she learned that true fulfillment and hope come from the inside through a relationship with Jesus Christ.

Her passion is to share what she has learned with all of those who are still looking for inner happiness and who believe that by changing their circumstances, they will eventually be satisfied. She wants them to know that the Lord Jesus is the only one who can truly satisfy and fill the void in their lives. While she experienced many valleys and dark places, she realizes now that God allowed these circumstances to show her how much she needed Him and that her own strength and determination would eventually fail her. It is her hope that anyone who reads her story may see themselves in it and realize just as she did that God is not far away.

In this book, our mother artfully shares her thoughts, emotions and questions through every stage of her life as she perceived them at the time. At the end of each chapter, there is a Bible verse which reflects her new understanding and perspective of God's heart towards her during those periods in her life.

Her story was written by our mother along with her daughters: my sister, Carol and me. As we finish up the final manuscript for this book, our mother is almost eighty years old. After so many years, she could not remember everyone's name, nor could she remember exact conversations. Nevertheless, she has done her best to reconstruct conversations and details. With the exception of immediate family members, we have changed the names of people, places, and businesses to protect their privacy. Finally, we hope we did not inadvertently hurt anyone's feelings in the process of writing this memoir.

*****

"From one man he made every nation of men, that they should inhabit the whole earth; and he determined the times set for them and the exact places where they should live. God did this so that men would seek him and perhaps reach out for him and find him, though he is not far from each one of us." Acts 17: 26-27

"Where Do I Come From?"

I come from a loving family
I come from a small town in Germany
I also come from a larger town where bombs destroyed our homes
I come from a country that went through a terrible war
I come from a place where hope never dies
I come from a mountain village where wood crafting is a special art
I come from a place where my father used to perform in an orchestra
I come from a situation after World War II where my mother did not know what to give us to eat because food was so scarce
I come from a place where life is always worth living even in adversity
I come from giving thanks to God for protecting our family
I come from always seeing the glass half full, instead of half empty
I come from loving the arts, appreciating great music, and being thankful that my family and friends enrich my life.

(written in October 2008, 53 years after I left East Germany)

PART I

GROWING UP IN GERMANY

—1—

Fleeing My Homeland

I remember the day I fled East Germany so clearly. It was the beginning of December in 1955, ten years since the war ended. I was 23 years old.

As I contemplated my illegal escape from East Germany for those few weeks before I left, I was in torment. I had never done anything illegal in my life before; the fear of the consequences was overwhelming. I just couldn't even let myself think about it. Throughout the war, I got very good at putting frightening thoughts aside and choosing to think hopeful and optimistic thoughts. As a teenager, I had fallen in love with a young man named Heinz, who had already left Germany forever. We still corresponded by mail each week and my love for him just continued to grow even though we were physically separated. In my heart, I wanted to follow him and marry him, but I also felt responsible for my family.

Although my father, Herbert, had returned from the war two years after it ended, I helped support my family and helped my

Mama, Gertrude, care for my youngest siblings: my sister Erika, who was 11 years old, and my brother Karl-Heinz, who was only 5. I lived with my family in Frohburg, a small town in Saxony, then East Germany, with a population of about 5,000 people. My job was in Boehlen, a small city, commutable by train from Frohburg. I worked in the quality control department for a company that made building materials. When I left my hometown, I did not officially quit my job; I just did not show up to work again. Strangely, it was not so unusual at that time for people to disappear. Some moved to other parts of Germany to reunite with family; others were like me, who wanted to try to leave the country. I worried whether anyone would contact my Mama after I left.

Heinz had escaped five years earlier, in 1950. He didn't try to escape through Berlin, like I did. There were many borders between East and West Germany that were patrolled by Russian guards and dogs, mostly German Shepherds. Heinz chose to run across a section of the border that didn't seem to be too heavily guarded. I do not really know where he crossed the border.

The first time Heinz tried, he ran across when he thought the guard had taken a break. But the guard saw him, caught him, and put him in a detention cell for a few days. The next day Heinz tried again, and he was successful. He just kept running until he was sure he was safe.

Terror gripped me when I learned what happened to him the first time he tried to flee, so I decided to ask the East German government for permission to visit a fictitious person in West Germany, hoping I would be permitted to leave and not have to deceive anyone at the border. When my request was denied, I feared that I was being watched by the government. At that point, I knew what I had to do and just decided to leave. However, I was NOT going to run across a border the way Heinz had. No, I would have to do this by deceiving the guards at one of the checkpoints. I heard stories of people who were able to escape this way. I wondered if I could actually pull it off. It was so foreign to my nature that I feared I would somehow betray myself. However, these were not ordinary times and something propelled me to move forward.

That morning, my sister Renate and I reviewed the action plan. Although Renate was 3 years younger than me, she was more organized and had a stronger, leader-type personality. We looked alike in some ways—we both had high cheek bones and a wide, pointed nose—yet I was much heavier and dark-haired, whereas Renate was slim and blonde. I was the oldest of five siblings, and my Mama had always depended on me to help with the little ones and help pay the expenses with my earnings. My father had no idea how to manage money, so we always had a problem. I loved him so much anyway; I chose to ignore his faults. I loved my entire family. But I wanted to be with Heinz—and so I mustered the courage to do what I had to do that day. I left because I was in love and because, even though it had been 10 years since the war ended, life was still so hard for the East Germans. Many people did not have good jobs. Even if they did have a job, they could not buy really quality food, furniture, paint, or even decent shampoo. I wanted a better life.

Renate and I knew our former neighbor from Frohburg, Frau Herta Fischer, now lived in East Berlin and had a sister-in-law on the western side of Berlin. We could not take a chance by writing to her, in case my correspondence might be opened by the East German officials. So, Renate and I planned to go to her apartment in East Berlin and hoped that she would be willing to help me get to the western side of Berlin.

That morning, my heart was very heavy. In my family's one-bedroom apartment in Frohburg, I started to say good-bye to my family members. First, I walked over to Karl-Heinz, my five-year-old brother, who we called Karli. I picked him up while he was still sleeping, cradled him in my arms, and kissed him good-bye. He had a sweet round face and dark brown hair. He did not wake up or even move as I cradled him. Next, I walked towards Erika's bed. Erika was 11 and looked exactly like me: we were both short and stocky, with high cheek bones and thin brown hair. Erika woke up, stood up in her bed, and she put her arms around my neck as tightly as she could. "Don't go, Anita. Stay here!" wailed Erika. Erika's hands were squeezing my neck so hard, I was afraid to move. We were both crying.

"I love you, Erika," I said.

Then I said, "Erika, don't tell any of your friends what I am trying to do. If I am successful, you won't see me again for a very long time. But if I am caught, I wouldn't want anyone to know that you knew about this." I said this just the way a mother would if she were warning her daughter of some potential danger.

Years later, Erika wanted to study foreign languages at one of the universities in East Germany. She had become fluent in Russian and English while she was in high school. She was exceptionally gifted and had planned to become an international translator and hoped to travel. But because of my actions on that day, the East German government did not allow Erika to pursue that career.

My other brother, Hans, was eighteen years old and studying to become an electrical engineer at the University in Mittenwalde, a small town in East Germany. Hans was very handsome, with brown hair and strong features; he was also the tallest member of our family, close to six feet tall. He did not know about my plans, and I never had the opportunity to say good-bye to him.

Then I walked out of the bedroom into the kitchen to say farewell to my Mama. This was the hardest good bye for me. My mother understood how much I wanted to be with Heinz, but my mother needed me there too, although she would not hold me back. I just hugged my Mama and didn't say anything. We had talked about it all before. We held onto each other for a few minutes, neither willing to be the first to let go. Then I began to tremble with fear. At that moment, I wished I could be that happy little girl again who loved to play in the park. My Mama didn't say anything, but I knew the love and support she was communicating.

My Mama then reached for her handkerchief inside the pocket of her smock and wiped her eyes with it as we began to walk outside. My Mama looked so vulnerable: she was petite, slim, and delicate, with a very small frame. She was wearing a thin pink smock dress with a white collared shirt underneath. She had only three outfits, and she wore them over and over again. I knew that my Mama supported my decision. My Mama hoped my marriage would be better than her own. My Papa adored my Mama, but my Mama had such a hard time with my Papa because he had no idea how to manage money. My mother had always been a mother first, and then a wife. My Papa was always bothered by that.

Renate understood how difficult this was for me. She carefully and gently suggested that it was time to go. We knew it would be some time before we would see each other again. Even if I were granted citizenship in West Germany, it would be too dangerous for me to travel back to East Germany. But no one could have imagined that it would be 20 years before I would see any of my siblings again. The next time I saw my brother Karli, he was a grown man, age 25.

Finally, I said, "Renate, I guess we should start. I am really scared, but I am so thankful to you for being willing to go all the way to Berlin with me."

"Anita, write to me as soon as you get across the border, so I know you made it safely," said my Mama.

"Ok, Mama. I will." I felt a grief and deep pain that I couldn't even put into words. I did not know if I would ever see my mother again. Even though I felt I was doing what was right for me, at that moment, the reality of the step I was about to take hit me with full force.

I was wearing all that I could possibly take—two dresses, two slips, one pair of undergarments, and two pairs of socks. It was a cold day. I also had a gray coat with large black buttons and a black woolen scarf that my Mama had knitted. I could not really take anything else along, and at least the scarf would be a little reminder from home. Renate had also worn two dresses with the intention of giving one to me so I would at least have three outfits until I could find work—that is, if I could successfully get to West Germany. The dress that Renate wore over her own was one of mine. It was a heavy blue dress with long sleeves and pockets, too big for Renate, but manageable with Renate's own dress on underneath.

I turned around again to wave good-bye to my Mama who stood by the apartment door and watched us walk towards the train station. She watched until we walked along the street up a short hill and turned the corner.

As we walked to the train station, I met my Papa, who was walking home from the train station after playing music with his band the night before. When we saw him, we stopped. My Papa was wearing his long black coat and black gloves, and he smelled of smoke. He had round thick glasses, brown hair, and was stocky. He was only a little taller than me, and I am not even five feet tall.

My Papa knew what I was planning, but he never understood, not the way my Mama did. "Your mama told me that you are really going to go through with this?" my Papa posed as a question. "Yes Papa, I am going," I said. My Papa nodded and looked down. After a brief pause, Papa said to me, "*auf der Suche nach deinem Gluck musst du deine Heimat verlassen?*" "Must you leave your homeland in order to find happiness?" I still remember his exact words. Those words shrunk my heart to the size of a pea. "Yes, Papa, I want to try. But I want you to know how much I love you," I said. I said that because I did not want my Papa to feel bad about my decision. He reached his arms completely across my body and hugged me. We both cried softly for a few minutes. Without another word, he let go, and we said good-bye.

I loved both of my parents very much. But for my father, there was always a very special place deep inside my heart.

Renate and I had to walk about two more kilometers (a little over a mile) to the train station in Frohburg. Neither of us talked much as we were walking. My mind jumped from feelings of fear, guilt, and excitement, like three channels on a television constantly getting switched. When we arrived at the Frohburg train station, Renate was careful to buy two round-trip tickets to Leipzig and two more round-trip tickets from Leipzig to Berlin. We were not going to take any chances and arouse suspicion. Even though neither one of us ever did anything like this, we thought through every detail very carefully and had rehearsed the plan over and over again to be sure that we weren't missing anything that could give the plan away. Fortunately, we did not wait long to get on the train to Leipzig, another large industrial city in Saxony.

When we got off the train at Leipzig, it was around lunchtime, and Renate had packed some rolls and butter that we ate while sitting on a bench in the train station. As we sat and ate, I momentarily let go of my fear. "Anita, this will work out for you," said Renate. "And don't worry about Mama; I will take care of the family now. You have an opportunity to be free, and you should try it. I know how much you love Heinz." Like my mother, my sister understood why I wanted to leave. Renate was already dating Roland, the man she married a few years later. Renate was already living on her own and working in Chemnitz, then called Karl-Marx Stadt, one of the largest cities in Saxony. Both she and I still referred to the city as Chemnitz; we could not get used to referring to it as Karl Marx Stadt, named after the great communist thinker and leader.

When we boarded the train at Leipzig, I walked silently and pensively as Renate reminded me that she would do the talking if anyone asked why we were traveling to Berlin. Fear took hold of me again. We were so different: I was the romantic one, I suppose like my Papa, and Renate was the practical, organized one, just like my Mama. When it came to implementing a carefully developed plan, Renate was the leader, I was the follower and we worked beautifully together.

This train was crowded, so we were glad to get seats next to each other. We were careful not to talk about our plans. You didn't know who would be sitting near you and we couldn't take a chance of being overheard. East German police were always walking around, suspicious of everything and everyone. That was one of the things I really hated about East Germany. When I thought of being free of that constant monitoring, my resolve was strengthened. Instead of talking about the only thing we really had on our minds, we talked of Christmas and how it would be so much fun for Karl-Heinz this year now that he was five years old.

"Our Karli will have such a nice Christmas this year. He is hoping the *Weihnachtsmann*[1] will bring him some chocolate," said Renate. A few miles before we reached Berlin, the train came to a surprising stop in an open area. East German police wearing dark blue uniforms and hats got on the train and started checking everyone's identification cards and tickets. "Let me see your papers, Fraulein," one said to us as he walked towards our seats.

"Here they are," said Renate.

"Very good. And what are you two doing in Berlin today?"

"We are going to visit Frau Fischer. She used to live in Frohburg near us, but after the war, she moved to Berlin. She lives on Malmoer Strasse. Since she has not been feeling well, our mother asked us to look in on her," Renate said, calmly and confidently.

"Ok then," said the guard. Renate made it seem so easy – I never could have pulled that off without my voice quivering and uncertainty in my eyes giving me away.

This same line of questioning went on with each of the passengers on the train.

Finally, the tortuous hour was over, and the train started up again.

"Well, Anita, everything is fine," said Renate. "We will be getting....

"Berlin, Berlin," yelled the conductor, interrupting Renate's sentence. Everyone, including the two of us, got off the train. We had never been to Berlin before. First, we went to the bathroom at the train station because Renate noticed that my face was red, swollen, and moist from sweating. We washed our faces and then walked around the train station to see if we could find a map. We realized the map was not much help, since many of the streets must have been renamed just like they were in Frohburg: for example, Strasse der Roten Armee (Street of the Red Army) was the main road in Frohburg. Maps with the new street names were not yet printed. Finally, Renate just asked a woman if she knew how to get to Malmoer Strasse. The middle-aged lady had a kind face and dark hair, and she answered, "Ja, it is not far from here." She gave us directions, and we walked there.

Now that we were in Berlin, I became very serious. I felt like someone was choking me, my fear was so heightened. I did not want to joke about Karli anymore. Renate assured me, "Oh, Anita, it is going to work, just wait and see." How could she be so confident? As we followed a road towards Frau Fischer's house, we noticed that most of the homes in Berlin had been rebuilt. Since Berlin was the capitol of East Germany, the Russians must have made the restoration of Berlin a priority. In Chemnitz, many houses were still awaiting repairs, and some neighborhoods had not even been rebuilt. It made me wonder how long it would take to rebuild the places where we were from. Yet even in Berlin, the buildings were a dark gray, dreary color. From the pensioners and other people who were allowed to move freely between East and West Germany, we knew that West Germany was very different. In East Germany, purchased goods were all rationed, even food. Most people in East Germany did not have telephone service, unlike West Germany, where almost everyone did. Many East Germans still did not have indoor plumbing. Because of the frequent comparisons to West Germany, East German residents were dissatisfied, disillusioned, and frustrated.

Without much talking, we walked arm in arm towards Frau Fischer's apartment. It had been about 5 years since we saw Frau Fischer, yet we were certain she would remember us. People were becoming so suspicious of each other, that sometimes you did not know who you could trust. Somehow, we knew Frau Fischer would be one of those people we could include in our circle of trust. Besides that, we didn't know anyone else in Berlin so we had to take the risk.

We arrived around 3 pm in the afternoon and knocked on her door. Frau Fischer answered and was completely shocked to see us.

"What are you two doing here, Renate and Anita? Is everything OK with Gertrude, Anita? Please come in, please."

Frau Fischer was a kindly older woman, about 70 years old, very tall and thin, and very energetic. She had short gray hair and was wearing a dark dress with long sleeves. Her one-room apartment had a small table, a sofa bed, a stove, and a sink. "Well, Frau Fischer, we couldn't take a chance by writing to you.... Anita wants to leave East Germany. We remembered that you had a sister-in-law in West Berlin and thought you might be able to help Anita get to the West," said Renate, without even stopping to breathe in between her words. What would Frau Fischer say?

Frau Fischer had been our neighbor in Frohburg for many years before she decided to move to Berlin. She often gave my Mama money or food when we needed it. She had been a very good friend. I just hoped that she did not change in the years she was in Berlin. "Are you going to go to America to marry Heinz, Anita?" asked Frau Fischer in an upbeat manner. "If I make it, I hope so," I said, as I stared at the floor. I had no idea that she was aware that Heinz had left East Germany.

So Frau Fischer agreed to help me. She was the type of person who would not let anyone push her around. She told me she was more than willing to take on this challenge. She took a few minutes to think about what to do while she directed us over to her round kitchen table.

After a few minutes, she told us, "I think the best way to do this is for me to take the Underground to West Berlin. I am a pensioner, so they won't ask me any questions. I'll talk to my sister-in-law. In the meantime, you two stay in my apartment until I come back. Let me pack a bag and take the extra clothes that you have on over there now." You could see the wheels turning in her mind as she was thinking through what the best option would be. We also knew that we did not have more than a day to work everything out because they would probably start inquiring about my whereabouts from work.

So my sister and I took off the extra dresses that we had each put on and helped Frau Fischer pack them in a little black bag. Frau Fischer then put on her gray coat and hurried out the door.

To me, it seemed like many hours, but in reality, Frau Fischer was gone for only a little while. When she walked backed in, I hoped that the news was good. Frau Fischer had a big smile on her face. "I talked to my sister-in-law, and she will help you, Anita. You can spend the night with her, and she will give you West German marks so you can fly out of West Berlin right away and go to Frankfurt. She will also give you enough money to help you for the first few days and for the train," she said. I was completely overwhelmed and did not know what to say. Her sister-in-law did not even know me. Why would she take a risk to help me?

West Berlin was completely surrounded on all sides by East Germany, so the only way to get out of West Berlin without having to cross through East German borders and guards again was to fly out.

Frau Fischer waved a brown paper bag in Renate's direction. "Here, Renate, this is for Karli and Erika. It is some good German chocolate from West Berlin, not like the chocolate made with sand that we get here. My sister-in-law wants you to have this. Also here is some good-quality coffee from West Germany for your Mama. Please take it back to her."

"Anita, I think the best thing for us to do is to cross over from East Berlin to West Berlin by walking across the Bornholmerbruecke on Invaliden Strasse. That large bridge crosses over railroad tracks, and it connects the Russian zone in East Berlin to the French zone in West Berlin. From there, it is only a short trolley ride to my sister-in-law's apartment. My sister-in-law's name is Frau Hildegard Schiller."

Frau Fischer continued, "What we will tell the guards when we cross the bridge is that you and I need to take a bath over there. They know most East Germans do not have bathtubs. We'll carry towels across our arms. I'll do the talking, don't worry about anything." It was all arranged. I gladly allowed the confident Frau Fischer to make the decisions. We then walked back to the train station so we could see Renate off. As much as I knew this moment would come, I did not want Renate to leave. She was my last connection to my family. I wanted her to give a good report to my Mama so she would not be worried so much.

"At least you can tell Mama that everyone is helping me. As soon as I can, I will write to Mama to let her know if I made it," I said. I didn't even let myself think about what would happen if I did not make it. I hoped I was doing the right thing.

Renate and I hugged for a few timeless minutes. Tears flowed down both of our faces. No other words were necessary. We understood each other without having to speak any words. Renate then quickly walked down the stairs to the train platform and waved good-bye.

Then Frau Fischer and I walked back to her apartment to get some towels. Next, we began to walk toward Bornholmerbruecke. "Now remember, Anita, we will tell the guards that you and I need to take a bath over there," said Frau Fischer. She placed the towels on top of her bag so they would be visible to the guards. "We'll tell the guards that we haven't had a bath in over a month," joked Frau Fischer, hoping to get me to loosen up a bit. "Do not worry, Anita. These guards are just little boys who think they have a little bit of power. We can handle them today," she said. Her voice was strong and commanding. As we continued to walk and got closer to the bridge, I know the color must have left my face. I felt lightheaded. My legs felt heavy. I asked Frau Fischer to stop a few times as we were walking so I could catch my breath. I had a sharp pain on my right side. My back was wet from perspiring, and I felt my heart pushing against my chest.

As we approached Bornholmerbruecke, we saw many guards occupying the middle of the bridge. The East German guards wore dark blue uniforms, the same ones the police on the train had worn.

I remember Frau Fischer explaining, "These East German boys who become border guards are given extra time off and some extra food rations for doing this job. They act just like the Nazi Gestapo once did. Didn't they learn anything from this war?" We started to walk across the bridge, and when we got about halfway across, a young guard stopped us by holding up his hand and blocking our path. "Where are you going? How long will you be there? What is the purpose of your visit?" The blonde guard on the bridge on the East Berlin side was probably only 20 years old – just a little younger than I was. My mouth was dry from the nervousness I was feeling. My throat was closed. I could not answer. My heart was pounding so hard, I could feel it pushing against my chest. My clothes were sticking to my back from the nervous sweat. I just looked down. I could not meet his eye. What I was about to do was so against my nature, yet from somewhere within, I was determined to try. Frau Fischer answered the guard. "We need to take baths at my sister-in-law's apartment. We will walk back before it gets too late."

"Where do you live?" asked the guard. "Isn't there anyone near you who has a bath?" he continued.

"No," Frau Fischer answered, "We take baths at my sister-in-law's apartment in Berlin."

"OK, you may pass," said the young blonde guard, "but you better return by this evening, or there will be trouble."

You have no idea, I thought. I just hoped the guard was not looking at me. I felt the sweat trickle down my backside. I could not wait to pass him and get to the other side. We walked a few more meters. The guard on the western side just waved and smiled at us. He never said a word. I did not dare look back. Each step was heavy but deliberate. As we got closer to the other side, I felt the breeze cool my face. Freedom was only a few steps away, I thought. After a few more minutes on the bridge, I had crossed over to the other side. We were in the French zone and in West Berlin. I could not believe we had done it. I fought back tears.

With each step, I gained confidence and began to breathe more evenly. We were safe. I felt so relieved, but I was still scared. Even though we did it, I was still fearful of the future: a future that I could not even imagine - but I had taken a very important first step.

*****

"For I know the plans I have for you", declares the Lord, "plans to prosper you and not to harm you, plans to give you hope and a future." Jeremiah 29:11

—2—

Why I Left: for Love—and a Better Life

I met Heinz in the summer of 1947 when I was fifteen and he was seventeen. I asked my Mama if I could enroll in a dancing school, and she agreed. There was not all that much for young people to do after the war. When this dance company announced it was coming to Frohburg, I was really excited. The company used the Frohburg Schuetzenhaus (a small dance hall and restaurant) for the lessons. The Schuetzenhaus was a gray building, partially hidden by the forest trees that surrounded it. Really, it was like a country inn with a dance floor. Unfortunately, I had only one dress, and I had to wear it over and over again.

When I started dancing school, I noticed Heinz right away. He was a good-looking man with the bluest eyes and the most beautiful dark brown hair I ever saw. I thought he was so handsome. Since he was only 5’4” tall and I am only 4’11,” we made a nice dancing couple. He was shy, and that also attracted me to him. I think my bubbling personality made Heinz feel at ease, too.

As each week's lesson went by, I became more and more excited to go to these dancing lessons. I started to come early, hoping that Heinz would do the same. After a few weeks, Heinz asked me to go to the café to get a cup of coffee and cake afterwards. My girlfriends winked at me as Heinz and I walked over to the café. I noticed that Heinz also looked so neat. His shirts were clean and tucked in: I could tell that he took care of his things. But he also had only a few outfits to wear, and like me, he wore them over and over again. As he spoke, I felt my heart warming towards him. When he walked me home, Heinz always picked up any debris along the stone pathways. When we got near the bakery, he went inside to throw out what he had collected. When we arrived at my family's apartment, he gently kissed me on the cheek before opening the apartment door for me. I thought my cheeks were burning and my skin was electrified. I thought this must be what love feels like.

The next week, Heinz asked me to take a walk after the dance class was over. We walked to the lake in Frohburg, called Schlossteich. There were beautiful mature trees all around the lake. Birds chirped and the sun brightened the lake. There was a concrete wall that we sat on, and we took turns picking up and throwing pebbles into the water. We watched them skim across the lake and then disappear into the water. We were very relaxed with each other. Neither one of us was in any rush to get home.

Heinz talked about how much he liked the man he was working for in Geithain, another small town in Saxony. He was an apprentice for a cabinet maker. “My boss let me make a toy rocking horse for my younger brother Winfried. I made it from the wood scraps. I also made a doll’s crib for my little sister, Christa.” I am going to give it to them for Christmas,” Heinz exclaimed, with a big smile that revealed the large space between his two front teeth. I was touched by his thoughtfulness and love towards his siblings.

Other times, Heinz asked me to go to the movies with him. There was one movie theatre in Frohburg, called Der Rote Hirsch (The Red Deer). The movies were so much more exciting than just listening to the radio and the theaters were dark and we could snuggle together while we watched the show. We always had fun no matter what the movie was. In the summer, we walked to the lake after the movie was over and spent time just walking and talking about life and looking up at the multitude of stars. Somehow, being with Heinz and seeing the stars made me feel so full of hope and that anything was possible.

I did not go to his home all that often; usually, he came to our apartment and talked to my family. Heinz was very comfortable with my Mama. My Mama always gave Heinz a cookie or something sweet to eat. Sometimes my Mama made her own butterscotch candies, by heating butter and sugar together over the stove. They tasted buttery and Heinz really liked them. He also liked playing with my younger sisters and brother and they loved it when Heinz came over. I thought Heinz would make such a good father when I saw him playing with Hans and Erika.

One time, I remember that Heinz invited me to dinner at his family's apartment, which was near the marketplace in Frohburg, on Kleinegasse Street. They had a third-floor apartment. His parents seemed very nice. His mother, Marta, was short and stocky, with brown hair and hazel eyes. Her hair was pulled up, and her lips always looked puckered. She looked tired, too, probably from taking care of Christa, who was just a baby. Heinz's dad, Paul, was a pleasant man, slender and also very handsome. He and Heinz had the same mannerisms, the way they walked, the way they tilted their heads at an angle towards you if they were trying to make an important point. But Paul was quiet and hardly said anything the entire evening, so I never really got to know him. Marta warmly invited me to join them at the table. The meal was meager, just potato soup and bread, but it filled us up and we didn't go to bed with a hollow empty feeling in our stomachs.

After dinner, Marta tended to the baby, while Heinz, Winfried, their father, and I sat on the sofa in their apartment. Winfried was seven years old: he was a small brown-haired boy and very sweet. He did not look very much like Heinz. Later, when Winfried went to bed, Heinz showed me the wooden toy horse he had made for Winfried. It was perfectly made, all natural with details carved into it, not painted. I could tell Heinz was very proud of it. I thought it was so nice that he was so kind towards his younger brother. "Oh

Heinz, Winfried's imagination will just ignite as he plays with this horse and his other toys," I said. Since Heinz was ten years older than Winfried, I believe that Heinz felt protective of him.

Often, Heinz and I talked about the war. Heinz was originally from Schlesien, the most eastern part of Germany at the time; today, it is part of Poland. His family settled in Frohburg in the beginning of 1945 after leaving their homes to avoid the oncoming Russian troops. Heinz explained one night as we were walking around Frohburg, "I remember when we had to leave Schlesien. We did not bring too much with us. But my grandparents did not want to leave. They decided to stay there, but my father thought it would be safer for us to move closer to the middle of Germany, and so we settled in Frohburg. I was very upset about leaving my grandmother behind. My grandmother said to me, "now come on my Soehnchen [in dialect, it means little son], you go ahead with your father".

"I still did not like it, but I went along with my dad. A few weeks later, as the Russian troops started to take over the area, my grandparents decided to leave, but by then, it was too late. As they walked away from the village, my grandmother had a heart attack along the road. After hours of digging, my grandfather just buried her right there. After that, my grandfather was so distraught that he went back to Schlesien. He is still there."

Heinz's face turned tomato red when he talked about his grandmother. I did not know what to say. Later, I learned that his grandmother had been like a mother to him and that is why he was so upset over it. But at the time, he did not share that with me. It was really hard for Heinz to talk about things that touched his emotions. He often just became quiet when the conversation moved in that direction.

Other times when Heinz and I would walk to Frohburg's Schlossteich, he talked about how so many people in East Germany could not find good jobs. Sometimes, Heinz talked of escaping and settling in America. I thought he was just a dreamer.....like I was. That time as he said good night, Heinz kissed me passionately.

After a year, we began to spend a lot more time together, and my Mama asked me what was going on. "You know, *Grosse*, I really like Heinz. He is a good man. Are you going to marry him?" "*Grosse*" is what my parents always called me. It means oldest child, and it is really a term of endearment.

"Oh, I don't know," I said, trying to hide my true feelings. Right then, both Renate and Hans started laughing.

"Why are you laughing?" I asked them, still trying not to give myself away.

"Oh, come on, Anita, you do nothing but talk about him, and we never see you anymore. You go to work, come home, and he meets you each evening. You two come here all the time. Then you come home late and collapse on your bed," said Renate. I realized that they were right and that I did want to spend the rest of my life with Heinz. But Heinz never talked about marriage, and he never made any commitments. We were also still very young.

When Heinz came to my apartment to pick me up, he always had a nice conversation with my Mama. Sometimes he brought flowers or coffee for my Mama, too. He was very much at ease with her. But my Papa and Heinz really had nothing in common. They had a cordial relationship that was all. Of course, my father was not home as much as Mama, but even when he was, my Papa and Heinz could never really find anything to talk about. It never occurred to me that this could be a red flag because in so many ways, I was just like my father....

One evening, I walked into our apartment and sat at the table in the kitchen with Mama. Mama heated up coffee on the stove and cut up a small piece of cake for me.

"Mama, do you think I should marry Heinz?"

"Ach, Anita, Heinz is a very practical man. He is responsible. He won't be like your father who doesn't know how to manage money. And he doesn't drink too much like your father sometimes does. I really think you will have a good life with him," said my Mama without any hesitation.

I had to admit that I was attracted to the stability that Heinz offered. I knew Heinz planned to become a carpenter. He was very skilled and very conscientious. Carpenters were in high demand in Germany because there was so much construction needed everywhere in Germany. I knew he would be able to find a good job with those skills. Later, my sisters Renate and Erika both married men who were very practical, men whom they thought would be good, stable providers. I guess none of us wanted to go through what our Mama went through, being married to a man who was loving but somewhat irresponsible and could not be counted on. But at the time, I certainly didn't see that at all. My father was my hero.

One summer evening in 1950, after we had been dating for three years, Heinz and I spent some time walking around Frohburg. It was a warm evening, and the town was very quiet that night. We held hands and walked along the stone pathways in Frohburg. When we came to Heinz's parent's apartment, we sat outside on a bench for a while.

"Wait here," said Heinz. He ran into his apartment and grabbed a box and brought it out for me.

"What is it?" I asked.

"Well, open it up. I had been hiding it in the building's basement," he said. While I opened it, I felt my face grow hot. I pulled off the tissue wrapping paper, and I saw that Heinz had made a square wooden jewelry box. It was simple, and yet so beautiful. He had hand-carved a rose on the top. He put a latch on it, too. He later made a small one for my Mama, too.

"Thank you so much, Heinz," I said. I was almost crying. It was just so special because he had made it himself.

"But why did you hide it in your basement?" I asked him.

"I didn't want Marta to see it," he said.

"Why not?" I wondered and could not really understand.

Heinz then told me that Marta, the woman married to his father, was not his birth mother. She was good to him and treated him fairly, but she could be manipulative and controlling. Heinz was an independent thinker from a young age and he did not trust anyone who tried to tell him what to do. Thus, he never really trusted or felt comfortable with Marta, so he never shared anything intimate about his life with her.

"Anita, I never even saw my real mother. If I did, I do not remember. My grandparents told me that she saw me once when I was two, but I have no memory of that. She was not married to my father, and when she realized that she was pregnant, she did not want me even though they gave me her last name at hospital where I was born. My father agreed to take responsibility. When I was born, my father's parents raised me. They lived on a farm. I lived with them until I was six. Then my father married Marta. After that, I lived with them." He stopped talking when his voice began to crack too much. I looked directly into Heinz's moist blue eyes. I thought he was the handsomest man I had ever met. I was sad for the hurt and rejection he must have experienced as a child.

After a few minutes, Heinz continued. "The day my father took me to city hall and officially took me as his son and gave me the Plutte name, well, that was the happiest day of my life. Marta had actually helped my father with all the paperwork." Before that, Heinz explained, he had his mother's surname for his own, even though she had given him up as a baby.

He must really love me, too, I thought, to trust me and share his feelings like that. Heinz's stepmother had always treated him well. In fact, Heinz's brother Winfried never knew that Heinz was only his half-brother while he was growing up. He was told only after he finished his schooling.

I often wondered if Heinz was teased or experienced prejudice because of this. He must have realized he was different when he started kindergarten. All the other children would have been living with both parents, while Heinz lived with his grandparents. I do not know how often he saw his father. I knew it was painful for him, so I never really asked, and other than the one conversation on that night, he never mentioned it again.

Heinz and I continued to spend all of our free time together, and he talked of escaping from East Germany. One evening after we both finished work, we were at the lake in Frohburg.

"Oh, Heinz, you are not really going to do that. They have the borders guarded now. It is too dangerous," I said. I thought he was dreaming. I never took it seriously.

"Anita, I am going to America. I have two uncles there, my father's two brothers. Once I get to West Germany, I can write to them, and one of them will help me get there. I do not want to stay here any longer. There is no opportunity here," he said. His voice was confident.

From what I remember, Heinz's father, Paul, stayed in Germany because his own father, whose name was August Plutte, did not want to lose all three of his sons, so he asked Heinz's father to stay. August's other two sons, Fritz and Wilhelm, had gone to America after World War I. So I guess Heinz felt he would fulfill his father's dream, Paul's dream, of going to America. During and after the war, Heinz's two uncles supplied their family with clothes and food. He never really told me what his parents thought about his plans.

Still, I never believed Heinz would actually leave. After all, he had his family in East Germany. But a few days after that evening, I received a letter from Heinz. He was in West Germany: he had escaped. That was in the summer of 1950. He first got a job at a small farm, and later, he worked in the coal mines in Oberhausen Osterfeld, a city in West Germany, with a population of about 200,000. I was completely stunned when I got this letter. I thought to myself, this man does what he says he is going to do. Somehow, I believed I could really trust him. Heinz had never made any commitments to me and I was only 18 at the time. But at the same time, I was hurt that I was not involved in the details. I did not know if our relationship was over. So, I wasn't really sure how to respond. With guarded emotions, I wrote back and told him how happy I was for him.

To my surprise, Heinz wrote to me every week. From that, I knew he was determined to keep the relationship alive. I often visited Heinz's family in Frohburg and had dinner with them at times. One time, Marta very gently suggested to me that perhaps I should start looking for another boyfriend. We knew Heinz planned to go to

America. Marta doubted that he would commit to helping me get out of East Germany and ultimately to America. Paul even suggested that perhaps Heinz might have already found another girlfriend. Those words stung. I got so angry, I am certain I was red-faced; I stood up and told them with confidence that Heinz would wait for me. Looking back on it now, I realize they were trying to protect me from getting hurt. Also, I was so terrified of war, and never wanted to experience it again. I was attracted to Heinz because he was going to a country that I thought was untouchable. No war would ever occur on American soil, I thought.

Four more years went by. I worked and helped support my family. Heinz and I wrote to each other every week for all of those years. He said he wanted to marry me in those letters and that I should follow him once he got to America. I could not imagine that he would actually get to America. Somehow I thought he would return or perhaps settle permanently in East Germany. I just wanted to know what happened to him and I was hoping that it would turn out that we could be together.

Finally in March 1954, Heinz's dream became a reality, and he greeted the shores of America. Once Heinz was in America, he became very serious about our relationship because he now felt that he could provide for our life together, and he asked me to join him there. I was so conflicted. I loved him so much more than anyone else I ever met. He needed me and wanted me and I so desperately wanted to be together with him. I was also terrified to leave. Many people tried to escape and many people ended up in jail or returning. The government did not treat people who tried to escape very kindly. What if I would get caught? How long would I have to be in jail? I might never see Heinz or my family again if I weren't successful.

Also, I did not want to leave my family behind. I was the oldest and felt like my mother's best friend and right arm in taking care of the family. Things had gotten worse at home with my father's drinking. I was an adult and my mama depended a lot on me. My earnings helped my family. We had been through so much together, and I actually ached inside when I thought about the sorrow they would feel and I would feel when we were separated. It was very likely we might never ever see each other again. Three conflicting emotions pulled at me: my intense fear of being unsuccessful in my escape, my sense of obligation to my family, and my desire to be free and with Heinz.

Here is one of the letters Heinz wrote to me:

6.30.55

Dear Anita,

Ach, I have so much to write to you. But first, I need to tell you the most important thing. Look, I just thought that perhaps I should ask your parents if they have anything against our plans, and if they agree that you should leave, I promise that I would marry you as soon as possible. I thought I would ask you first to see what you think. Then I would like to know from you, if you agree, what I should ask your parents. And if you think so, please write exactly for me what I should say. I thought about everything again, and I have to tell you the sad news that everything is now in your corner. But if we both just have a little more patience, then everything will be OK. You promised that you would come up with an answer.

Greetings and kisses from your,

Heinz

I thought it was so cute that he wanted me to tell him exactly what to say. He was very direct and honest in his communication but there was not a salesman's bone in his body. He knew he would have to persuade my parents to get them to give their blessing for him to take me away from my homeland. He knew how much they depended on me. I do not have the letters I wrote to him, but I must have written him back with a lot of excuses, like being homesick, and how hard it would be to leave.

Here is another letter he wrote to me:

Monday, 21.7.55

My Dear Anita,

I received your dear letter today and the beautiful card from Cursdorf. Naturally, I was very happy, and I thank you from the bottom of my heart. I was happy that you liked it there, and I hope had a relaxing time. When you take a few days of vacation, and you use them correctly, then future work will be so much easier to battle.

Now, dear Anita, I have to come back to question at hand, what I have postponed so many times. It is about us. You know you should never break anything over your knee [a German expression meaning to do hastily]; however, you also should not push it out too long. And the situation is at hand. I wrote you so many times how things are from my perspective, did everything in my power to smooth your way. Now it is your turn.

When you truly love me, as you said in your letters, should it not be a big deal for you, or are you just playing with me? I do not have any patience for that. Yes, Anita, I love you, and you know that. And I also know how good you are, and I will probably never find another woman with your qualities. However, when you are there and I am here, then one of these days someone else could take your place, not with your qualities, and you don't have to wonder one of these days, if that should happen. You can never retrieve anything in your life. Every day that is passed is lost, and you can never retrieve it again. And so we waste the best years of our lives. My dear Anita, I do not want to force you, I just want to make it clear to you, you know that you are old enough, and you don't have to hang on the apron strings of your mother. And the talk of homesickness, well, no one ever died from that. Now I want to tell you what I thought we would do if you decide to do something about the situation. It is so simple. You just take some clothes and just leave. And about other things, you don't have to worry about it. Here in America, we can't use those things anyway. Then I would leave some money for you at an address which I will tell you about later. And that should be enough until you find a job. And then I will write you more when the time comes.

Now, dear Anita, I believe I told you everything what is on my heart. I hope you are not too upset, but one time, you have to make a decision. Now I hope that you answer this letter without any excuses or delay. And then we will see how things develop.

I believe it is enough for today. I hope of a quick reply. Greetings and kisses from Heinz. I hope it is soon a reality, because kisses in letters lose their spice in the air.

His patience was wearing thin and I felt that Heinz was giving me an ultimatum with the last letter; so I knew I had to finally make a decision. I saw Heinz as a man who followed through on his word. I saw America as a haven. Things were not really getting better in Germany. True, we were no longer at war, but everyone still seemed to be afraid. Communism was taking over. The borders were guarded. People knew the West was prospering and our part of Germany was stagnating. I saw my Mama's disappointment with my Papa. As loving as he was, he made a very insecure home for our family. I believed that I would have a better life if I left and that

Heinz would be more responsible that my Papa had been. Yet, I was so tormented about this decision. Leaving my wonderful family was the most difficult—I felt so guilty about it. I spoke to my mama and she told me to make the decision. My father never understood and I knew he did not really approve. I loved Heinz and I really wanted a better life for my future children. So, I responded to his letter and said, yes, I will follow you to America.

It took about five more months until I was finally ready to go. In all that time, I had met only one other man that I was even attracted to. He was my colleague at the gasoline company, but he was already engaged, so I did not pursue it. I went out with other young men, but for some reason, there was always Heinz. I believed that Heinz and I were meant to be together. And I was attracted to the prospect of going to America: to me, America was untouchable. I assumed that once I got to America, all my problems would be gone and I would have a rosy life, without war or hunger or poverty or fanaticism. I couldn't wait to leave all those problems behind.

*****

"For He satisfies the thirsty and fills the hungry with good things." Psalm 107:9

—3—

The Innocence of Childhood Tainted by War

I was born in Frohburg, Germany in 1932 and was the oldest of five children. When I was two months old, my family moved to Chemnitz, which was a fairly large city in Saxony, Germany, with a population of approximately 250,000 today. My family rented an apartment on the bottom floor of a factory-turned-apartment building on Ludwig Strasse in Chemnitz. The apartment had only one bedroom and another large room that served as a kitchen and living room, with a stove that would heat into the living room, but the bedroom got very cold at night. In the winter, ice often formed on the walls and on the furniture. When it was that cold, my parents shared their bed with us, my parents on the outside and me, my sister Renate, and Hans in the middle. Sometimes my Mama put a hot water bottle in the bed, too. The bathroom, an outhouse, was outside.

My grandparents, my father's parents, rented the third floor of an apartment right along the same block, just around the corner.

Across the street, there was a park, with a sandbox and small fields to play in. There was also a bakery, a milk store, and Richter's small grocery store on the same block. On the next block, there was a soap store with all kinds of differently shaped soaps. I just loved smelling those soaps.

One of my earliest memories of my Papa is of him and I going to the Opera House in Chemnitz, called the Chemnitzer Opernhaus. My Papa was a very talented musician, and he played the trumpet in the house orchestra at the Opera House. I was often invited to go with him and watch the rehearsals. I just loved that. Before that, my Papa was a member of a band that performed at special events around the country. I went to those band rehearsals, too. Sometimes, the band conductor gave me a baton so that I could stand next to him and help him conduct the musicians. My Papa just beamed. I could see him smiling at me even as he played his trumpet, and I was so proud of the beautiful music he could play. The other musicians often talked to me after the rehearsals and told me what a wonderful musician my father was. I sensed that they admired his special talent.

My Papa also took me to all kinds of plays and musicals when I was a child. One time, when I was around five years old, he took me to see *Hansel and Gretel*. He said, "*Grosse*, let's go out tonight."

"*Ja, Papa, das mach ich gerne*." "Yes, Papa, I would love to do that," I said. And after the play, he took me across the street to a café to get some hot chocolate and cakes. As we sat at a small table in the café, I looked at my Papa's face and asked him to sing me a song.

"*Grosse*, I would love to, but singing is something I cannot do. Your Mama is the one with the beautiful voice," he answered.

It was true. When we went to sleep each night, my Mama always sang us a song. One of my favorites was a song that we had learned in our church, the Schlosskirche in Chemnitz. The song was called "*So nimm den meine Haende und fuehre mich.*"

My Papa let me sing it to him right there.

"So nimm den meine Haende und fuehre mich, Bis an mein selig Ende, und ewiglich. Ich mag allein nicht gehen, nicht einen Schritt, Wo Du wirst gehen und stehen, da nimm mich mit."

It means, "So take my hands and lead me until my blessed ending and until eternity. I do not want to go alone, not even one step. Take me with you, whether you go, or stop." I loved the music and always thought of my Papa when I sang that song; it made me feel at peace.

My Papa knew I was out much later than I should have been.

"*Grosse*, it is getting late. We better get back, or your Mama will be angry with me for keeping you out so late," said my Papa.

"Ach, Papa," I said, "Mama won't be upset. Can't we just walk along Chemnitz?"

"OK, let's walk and we will look at the stars. Then you tell your Mama that it was your idea to stay out so late," said my Papa, as he laughed with a twinkle in his eye. Some of my Papa's friends from the orchestra were in the café. They shook his hand and wished us good night. Then they asked my Papa who his young date was. We walked all around the town that night, admiring the stars.

I always felt as though my Papa understood me. He and I both noticed the good, beautiful, and pleasant things in life. We did not like to talk about anything hard or ugly. We loved getting lost in the beauty of the arts and nature, enjoying good food, and leaving all of our cares behind.

On the weekends, I would often sit on my Papa's feet while he practiced his trumpet. As his feet counted to the music, I would bounce up and down with him, and I could look directly into his trumpet. I often would wonder 'Where did that beautiful music come from?' My Papa also played the zither and the violin. I could listen for hours being carried away by the beauty of the music and my father's skill and making so many different types of instruments sing to me. I admired him, and as I got older, I never wanted to admit that he occasionally drank a little too much. As I matured, I had wonderful discussions with my Papa. We both loved music and the arts. We would talk about the operas, the characters, and how the music conveyed the emotions of the characters. We both loved the way music could express emotion in a way that words could not. In the music, I felt like the longings deep in my heart were understood in a way that I could never recreate any other way.

It was really wonderful to have my grandparents right on the same block. They were very involved in our lives. My grandfather went into town every Saturday morning. He always needed something— glue to fix his shoes or nails for a toy chest and coffee for my Mama. However, before he went out the door, he would give a few coins to me and Renate. With a smile and a laugh, he told us we could buy whatever we wanted for our sandwiches. Richter's grocery store, right across the street, was the place where my family bought our food. It always smelled so good there. The sweetness of baked goods, mixed with the aroma of fresh homemade soup still simmering on the stove, was intoxicating. When we walked in, Renate knew exactly what she wanted: little chocolate coins with jimmies on top. My eyes were focused on the many cheeses on display. I just loved cheese. That special cheese, shaped like a hotdog, was the one I chose. Then Mrs. Richter would put a few extra Toffee Candies in our bags. Our grandfather's eyes smiled and twinkled when we told him how we spent the money.

I loved basking in the warmth and love that I experienced with my grandparents. "Now I have a surprise for you, Anita and Renate," said my grandfather. We were always excited to see our grandparents. At the corner of the room, I noticed something that was covered with a white blanket. "What is under the white blanket, *Opa*?" I asked. (*Opa* is the familiar term for grandfather). "Well, come over here and take a look."

As I uncovered the surprise, with great delight, I saw a hobby horse. It had two seats, one on each side, and a handle in the middle for the two of us to hold onto. Both of us were so anxious to ride the horse, we climbed right on and started riding back and forth. Our grandfather beamed with joy.

In 1938, when I was six, I started attending school in Chemnitz. The first day of school is an important event for a German child, and the entire family celebrates this special day. That morning, when I started to get ready for school, I could not decide what to wear.

"What dress should I put on, Mama? Should I put my hair in braids?" I looked over at my Mama and realized even at that age what a truly beautiful woman she was. She was petite, with very small hands and feet, and very delicate facial features. She was only about 5' tall and she was thin. Her hair was curly brown and she had large beautiful blue eyes. My Papa told me that he decided to marry her the first day he met her.

"Anita, wear your new sweater and skirt. You look so nice in that skirt and I will put your hair up in a nice pony tail with a pretty bow so your hair will not fall into your eyes when you are working at your desk. I know you will have fun in school, but first, come into the living room. Your father, grandparents, and I have something for you," said my Mama.

As I walked out of the bedroom towards the living room, I saw everyone waiting for me with large smiles on their faces. Then I noticed that my mother was holding a long cone-shaped hollow cardboard container, decorated with wrapping paper. "Oh, my *Zuckertuete*" [Sweet Bag], I squealed with excitement. This is a German tradition. When a child enters school, her family presents her with the *Zuckertuete* on the first day. My Sweet Bag was mostly filled with chocolates and candy. But my grandmother had put cheese on the tip of the cone and wrapped it with aluminum foil so it would not interfere with the sweet aromas of the candies above it. "Do you like it?" asked my Mama, as she looked lovingly at me.

"Oh, Mama and Papa, thank you. I am so excited," I exclaimed.

"We are very proud of you, Anita," said my Papa.

"We know you will have a wonderful first day of school," said my Mama.

"Come along, *Grosse*. I will walk you to school today. After today, you will know the way," said my Papa. So I took my father's large thick hand, looked up at him, and started out of the apartment. The school building was just one block from the corner of Ludwig Strasse. It was called the *Grundschule* (elementary school).

When I got there, I met my teacher, Herr Zimmerman. He was a young man, maybe about 30 years old when I started school. He had a full beard and smoked a pipe. He was a bachelor, and everyone really liked him. When one of the students had a cough, he was always ready with a cough drop. Loose teeth were no problem: he volunteered to pull them out. He gave the children coins for their birthdays. He was my teacher for four years. Boys and girls were separated into two classrooms, and we had about fifteen girls in my classroom. I really enjoyed school; not just because of Herr Zimmerman, but because I loved to learn. When I learned to read, I felt like a whole world opened up for me and I could be transported far away from the growing fear in the world around me. Unfortunately after this point in time, my world would vacillate between the innocence of childhood and the evil and manipulation of the Nazism and the Third Reich.

That same fall, when I was still six, my grandmother and I took the trolley into the downtown part of Chemnitz to go shopping. As we were walking and we started to approach the main shopping area in Chemnitz, my mother stopped walking and just stared at the street in disbelief. We saw shoes and clothes that had been thrown into the streets. Broken glass from the smashed store windows was sprayed into the streets. I could not even begin to imagine what would have caused this. We have nice people in Chemnitz; who would do something like this? And WHY??? It just made no sense to me. I just could not grasp what happened. It was especially strange because it was not every store that was affected – only some of them. "Why did it only happen to certain stores?" I wondered. When my grandmother saw the vandalism and mess, she became very upset, actually scared. "Let's go home. These are all the Jewish businesses. I do not know why this happened here," she said. So we went right back home, and my grandmother never said another word about it. I tried to ask her what happened and why it only happened to the Jewish businesses, but she was afraid to even talk about it. I never saw my grandmother so frightened like that before, and I did not understand why. I also became intensely frightened, but the next day we had a picnic across the street in the park, and I forgot all about the scary shopping trip we had the day before.

Later, I learned that it was Kristallnacht. How could something so heinous have happened in my home town?

*****

In 1939, when I was seven, Adolf Hitler started World War II with the attack on Poland. I knew there was a war because we heard about it on the radio, but I did not really understand why. Everyone started to greet one another with "*Heil, Hitler*" by raising their right arm. No one said hello anymore, they always said "*Heil, Hitler*." In school, we were taught to greet adults by standing up straight and tall, raising our right arms, and declaring, "*Heil, Hitler*." We also sang "*Deutschland Uber Alles*" (Germany Above All) at the beginning of each school day.

My parents did not join the Nazi party: they didn't want to, and they weren't forced to. We never talked about why they didn't want to, but I could tell that my parents were not happy with the way things were changing in Germany. They always wanted us to know the good and honorable things about Germany like the great musicians, writers, artists, scientists and archaeologists that have contributed so much to world not just to Germany. Many of our neighbors, however, joined the Nazi party in order to keep their jobs. I wonder if they would have joined if they had a choice. No one talked about anything. For some reason, since my father was a musician, he was not forced to join the party. I never really understood that, but my father was thankful for the reprieve. From reading history, we know that school teachers had to join the Nazi Party and teach Nazi propaganda, otherwise they lost their jobs. I had no idea about this at the time. I guess that must be what happened to Herr Zimmerman. When I was in second grade, I remember one of these "lessons" in particular. "You must become strong and physically fit. Everything you do is for the Flag," said Herr Zimmerman to our class of 15 girls. I just dropped my head and looked at the floor. My face turned bright red.

"Roesch, is everything OK?" asked Herr Zimmerman. It was the custom to address the children by their last name.

"Ja," I responded, still not lifting my head.

Herr Zimmerman never asked me anything else that day. As Renate and I walked home that afternoon, I felt embarrassed all over again. I started to sob a little bit as I walked towards my family's apartment. It was beginning to rain, so we started to walk even faster. My Mama was outside with Hans (who was just a baby) in the wagon and saw me coming.

"What is wrong, Anita?" asked my Mama.

"Oh Mama, the teacher said everyone has to be strong and fit to be good enough for the Fatherland. I am so fat. I always come in last in the races," I answered my Mama, with intermittent sobbing.

"Don't worry about it, Anita. You are just fine. Everyone has different talents," said my Mama. Mama and I never talked about it again, but every day at school I was painfully reminded that I was not good enough and often the other kids would giggle when I struggled to keep up in the gym activities.

There were no Jewish children in my school. In Chemnitz, the Jewish people were now wearing the bright yellow star on their clothes, and when they walked by, they would step down into the street to let the other people, even children, pass by first. This made me very uncomfortable because I was taught that children should always honor adults, so I felt I should have moved out of the way for them. At the train stations and on pillars, I read signs "*Die Juden haben den Krieg gewollt.*" "The Jews wanted this war." It never made any sense to me. I did not understand the aggressive war that Germany was waging, nor could I have ever imagined what was happening to the Jewish population. My grandparents had a radio, so we learned bits and pieces of what was happening from them, but we never knew what was transpiring with the Jewish people. Only one time I remember that my grandmother said that one of the Jewish shop owners, whom she was friendly with, was missing. I also remember reading signs that said, "The enemy is always listening" on the billboards. It made everyone suspicious of one another. It was hard to trust anyone.

In 1940, when I was eight, Herr Zimmerman told all the children they had to sign up for the Hitler Youth. He said, "If anyone does not sign up for the Hitler Youth, I need a note from your parents explaining why."

So everyone signed up. At that point, all youth activities had to be organized by the Hitler Youth. Church choirs were still available, but you needed the approval of your Hitler Youth leader if you wanted to do that. I still sang with the church choirs, and I did get my leader to approve it. All other activities—whether singing, drama, or art classes—were organized by the Hitler Youth Groups. The next week, at the Hitler Youth indoctrination ceremony held in my school, all the youth promised, in unison, to be loyal to our *Fuehrer* and to our flag/fatherland.

Afterwards, my friends and I went to the first after-school meeting in our school classrooms and got our uniforms. I think it was a blue skirt and a white blouse. We also got black marching shoes. Pins were earned by performing well in the sport activities. So many points were awarded for each activity, like running, climbing, and jumping. A total of 180 points was needed to earn the first pin in sports. I was heavy and not very athletic and so I barely squeezed by, I got only 181 points. This was when I was in the *Jugendmaidchen* group, which is the group for "Young Girls." My youth leader, a fourteen-year-old girl named Heidi with long blonde braided hair, got me involved in acting and singing. Along with some other girls, I was selected to do dramas and choir concerts. Often performances were from the Saxony culture, many of them were Friedrich Schiller's plays. I was never shy about performing in front of people. I was only eight, but at that time, I thought I wanted to be an actress. I enjoyed singing and acting, and I knew I could hold the audience. I learned the lines quickly. My Mama could sing, but she was shy. I think she was surprised over my boldness.

At most of the meetings, our youth leader often explained that everything we did was for the Fatherland, and we should be thankful since Hitler had created jobs for everyone. Propaganda was always in the Hitler Youth songs, too. I cannot remember the songs, but they went something like this:

"Unsere Fahne flattered uns voran. ……….

Heute gehoert uns Deutschland und morgen die ganze Welt."

It means:

"The flag flies in front of us……….

"Today, we own Germany and tomorrow, the whole world."

This song was sung as we marched on some Saturdays, often in parades. The tune fit marching steps, thus no one really thought about the lyrics. That is why it was such a perfect brainwashing tool.

Afterwards, we did gymnastics outside the school building. At the young girls' meeting, Heidi often talked about the German Aryan race and how superior the Germans were to everyone else. After our meeting, the girls were allowed to go home, but the boys often stayed longer to practice shooting and to do more marching.

Later, meetings became more sporadic because the war was going badly. I am not sure now if I was not promoted to the next level, "*Jugend und Schoenheit*," meaning "youth and beauty," because I was not very athletic and I was more interested in singing with my church choirs, or because the meetings just started to fall off.

Beginning in fifth grade, I started at the *Hauptschule*. Herr Zimmerman recommended me, as it was only for the brighter children who had strong academic potential. Only two children from my grade (out of about 30 children) were selected. I hoped that at this school it might not matter so much how fast I could run. Even though the school was farther away, I could still walk there. The other kids stayed at the *Grundschule* until eighth grade. The *Hauptschule* was called *Heinrich Beck Schule*. It was a brick building with four floors and had a small playground. Around this time, too, the war got worse, and everyone had to do their part to help the "Vaterland". Food was rationed to families and my mother had to stretch our portion as far as she could since we had a relatively large family. Sometimes apples or cakes were distributed to the children at school. Even though I was just as hungry as everyone else, I never accepted the free food because I was fat. I was so self-conscious and didn't want to give anyone the chance to say anything about it or make fun of me. Inside, I died a little bit more every time I had to say "No thank you" when the treats were offered to us.

I was at that school from 1942 to 1944 (age 10 to 12).

One day, I came home from school and walked into our apartment to find my Mama howling like a wounded wild animal. She was sitting at the kitchen table, her head was down, she held her handkerchief clenched in her right fist. "Mama, *was ist los*?"

"Mom, what is wrong?" I asked. It was terrifying to see my Mama like that; she was always cheerful and strong no matter what happened. I couldn't imagine what would have happened to make her so inconsolable.

My Mama never answered me. She would not even pick up her head. I just put my arm across my Mama's back and cried with her for a while. When Papa came home, my Mama told him between sobs that her younger brother, Hans, had been killed. Hans was only 30. I remember that he was a soldier; I think he was in Africa, but I am not completely certain. Hans had been my godfather. My Mama and Hans were very close. Actually, he was a lot like my Mama. He was very kind and generous. Whenever we saw him, he always brought a little gift for us, a little toy, or some candies. He knew how much my Mama liked her coffee, so he always brought her some.

I was so upset about this. I dreamt of my Onkel Hans that night. I woke up several times, breathing heavily. Everything about the war and those days started to really scare me. "Why are we in this war?" I asked my Papa the next day. I think somehow it was important to me to understand what my uncle died for.

"*Grosse*, I wish I knew. It does not make any sense to me. I wish it would just end." That was not the answer I expected to hear. How could my favorite Onkel have died in this war and my parents don't even understand why we are at war? Instead, my Papa just changed the conversation to the opera that he was currently practicing for. It was *Fidelio*, an opera first produced in 1805 by Beethoven. It is the story about a woman named Leonore who disguises herself as a prison guard (Fidelio) in order to rescue her husband Florestan from certain death in a political prison. I remember him telling me how important his trumpet piece was in the opera as he started to practice his solo. We talked all about the opera, and we forgot about the war for a little while anyway.

Two years later, in September 1942, when I was ten, my father announced that he had to join the war. Renate was seven and Hans was five. I have no idea how much notice he was given. From what I remember, he came home one day, made the announcement, and the next day he left. He said he had to go to the Russian front. I wasn't really sure what that meant, but I cried and cried because I was afraid that my father would die in the war the same way my Onkel Hans did. We hardly had time to adjust – how could he find out one day and then have to leave the very next day?

After his announcement, my Mama busied herself with our dinner. She kept pulling her handkerchief out of the side pocket in her gray smock and wiping her eyes. I knew she was crying, but no one said anything more about it. I wanted to ask questions, but I could not find my voice because there was a huge lump in my throat. Instead, I just watched Renate and Hans draw on paper on the kitchen floor. When dinner was ready, we sat around the table and enjoyed the nice dinner of potato soup, bread, and pork roast that my Mama had prepared. Even though there was no conversation around the table, my mother was a great cook and that simple meal somehow made us all feel a little bit better. After dinner, my parents asked me to invite my grandparents to come over to our apartment. We all sat around the table as Papa played songs on his zither. My Papa often played the zither for us after dinner. Maybe he wanted us to believe that everything would stay the same and there was nothing to worry about even though we were all worried.

I still remember him playing the many folk songs from Saxony that night. One song really touched my heart. It is called, "*Das Feierabend Lied*." The song means, "The time in the evening when work is done, and the sun is slowly sinking and going to bed, and the night rises, then you have a quiet time because you enjoy nature and family around. Everyone puts down their tools. You are done with your work. It is a time to enjoy peace in the mountains in the evening." *Feierabend* is really a state of mind. It is a beautiful song, and I cried every time that my Papa played it. That night none of us had a dry eye. My Mama took her handkerchief out of her pocket, wiped her nose, and held it up to her eyes. One by one, we all started to cry. Even my grandparents were crying. I don't think I ever saw them cry before. Even though we didn't want the night to end, eventually we all went to bed. Our Papa left very early the next morning before any of us woke up.

After he left, I had no idea how bills were paid or how we had money for food, since my Mama did not have a job. I decided I would do whatever I could to help my Mama.

That Christmas of 1942 was the first time we celebrated without our Papa. It was very cold that year, so Renate and I went outside with a basket and collected twigs and sticks for our Mama to burn in the stove. When we got back to our apartment, our Mama had decorated the Christmas tree with cotton balls, string, and some hand-made paper rings that Renate and I had made the day before. Hans was very sick that Christmas, and my Mama did not have any medicine for him. She just boiled radishes and mixed the liquid with rock candy to make a sort of medicine for his cough. My Mama strongly believed in homeopathic medicine. Sometimes when Hans could not breathe, she rubbed butter on his chest, covered him up, and made him sweat. She thought that he would sweat out his cold.

At Christmastime, we had special toys that came out only at that time of year. My Mama tried to add to them each year. I had a dollhouse, and I was thrilled because the house had an actual sink in it. On the outside of the house, there was a little container that you could fill with water. There was a small metal pipe that came through the dollhouse, so that it seemed like water actually came through the faucet. Water actually came out in little drops. I was so proud of this.

I also had different-sized dolls. The smallest one was the size of my finger, and the largest one was about as big as my hand. The largest one was a porcelain doll that did not move. That doll just stood there, and I pretended that she cooked. That year, my Mama got some wool and made some clothes for my dolls. She made an apron for the porcelain dolls, and she made a little hat and a sweater for one of the smaller dolls. She made a blue blanket with little yellow dots (flowers) for the stroller in the dollhouse, too.

Renate's porcelain doll also got a new outfit, a blue skirt and a sweater. Her doll was the lady behind the counter in her small food store. That night, my Mama, Renate, Hans, and I huddled in bed together, with only a hot water bottle to keep us warm.

My Mama did the best she could to make Christmas feel like Christmas for us. No matter how hard she tried, the unspoken absence of Papa was impossible to escape. I kept wishing he would walk through the door on Christmas Eve, pick up his zither and accompany us as we sang Christmas carols. I could tell my Mama missed him too, but we never talked about it.

Shortly after Christmas, we learned where the bomb shelter, actually a basement in a nearby building, was located. The shelter was forty to fifty feet from our apartment. About twenty of us could fit, and we practiced running into it at night and in the dark so we would know where it was. At first, we just practiced as a family. My Mama wanted to make sure we knew where it was. Later, it must have been mandatory because I remember practicing with everyone in our apartment building when we heard the whirring sirens. Sometimes my Mama would bring a candle to help light the way.

A month later, we were not practicing anymore; we were often running into it at the command of the piercing siren. Our grandparents did not have a basement in their apartment building either, so they ran to the same shelter. As the war intensified, we often went to bed with some of our clothes on, so that we could dress more quickly and get there in less time. It started to feel normal to go to bed with our clothes on, but I found that it was harder and harder to fall asleep at night. The bomb sirens were so loud and frightening. It was terrifying to be startled awake by the siren and have to run as fast as you could into the bomb shelter. Mama told us not to worry about bringing anything with us. The most important thing was that we would all get there safely together.

There was also a young single woman who had a beautiful baby boy with blonde hair and blue eyes. I really liked her; she always smiled at me and our family. Yet, everyone gossiped about her. My Mama later told me that people guessed that she had had a child with a handsome Aryan man, just to please Hitler. She lived in our apartment building and ran with her infant, too.

In 1943, my Papa was given a two-week leave from the army and in this time, my sister Erika was conceived. On the last night before he had to return to war, he played the zither in the apartment for our family and some of the neighbors and my grandparents. We sat around the table and on the sofa while he played. I still remember the sweet emotional sound that the zither produced. One song stands out in my mind. It is called "*Saltzburger Glockenspiel.*" His little finger on his left hand just gently touched the zither to create the bell effects. It sounded like bells in the entire apartment. To me, it sounded like heavenly music. His music touched my soul. It made me feel like heaven opened up and the angels were singing. For that night, I just wanted to enjoy his music. Any thoughts of the war were pushed out of my mind. Unfortunately, he went back to the Russian front the next morning, and we all had to say our good-byes.

There was no longer a 'normal" in our lives. Schools were sometimes closed because of warnings of possible bomb raids. If we had school, we met in the basement of the building. By 1945, school had stopped altogether. In February 1945, Dresden, which was Saxony's cultural showplace, was bombed. Dresden's art museums, opera house, and the *Frauenkirche*, Dresden's famous church, were destroyed.

Our grandparents heard about the bombing of Dresden and informed my Mama. My Mama had already started to move us out of Chemnitz to get away from the city, where it would be safer. My sister Erika was now about eight months old, and my Mama wanted to protect her. My other grandmother, my Mama's mother, had a one-bedroom apartment in Frohburg, which was about 50 kilometers (or about 30 miles) from Chemnitz, more towards the center of Germany. We had little choice, so my mother started traveling back and forth with Erika and Hans to stay with her own mother. Renate and I traveled back and forth, too, but after Dresden was bombed, my Mama just wanted to keep us all in Frohburg. My Mama, Erika, and my grandmother stayed in my grandmother's apartment. Renate and I stayed with my Mama's sister. Hans stayed with a neighbor.

By this time, I was 13, my sister Renate was 10, my brother Hans was 8, and Erika was eight months old.

We were all in Frohburg when Chemnitz was bombed on March 5, 1945. My other grandmother, the one in Frohburg, heard about it on the radio. The very next day, my Mama and I went to Chemnitz to see if we could salvage anything from our apartment. I do not remember how we got there. I am sure the trains were not running. Farmers had wagons, maybe we got a ride that way, but I cannot remember.

When we arrived at Chemnitz, we could not believe what our senses were taking in. We smelled things burning, like chemicals. It made me feel sick. There was a thick dust blowing around. The streets were dirty from all the dust. Some streets were completely clear of debris, while others were covered with broken wood, chunks of concrete and shattered glass. No one was outside, and we had no idea where my grandparents had gone. Our apartment building and the building that my grandparents rented had been completely destroyed. We stood in the middle of the street, right in front of where our apartment had been. There was a mountain of wrecked dwellings, concrete, glass, wood, bits of cloth, debris, and dust. In the middle of the streets were smaller hills of demolished property. On the very top of one of these hills, I saw one of our white tea cups, upside down, yet intact. It was so strange. I picked up the cup, turned it around in my hand, and put it in my pocket to take back with us. That was the only item we saved from our apartment.

We carefully stepped around the broken glass and concrete on the streets and walked to the corner. Around the corner, other apartments were completely intact, and we wondered if people were still inside. We walked down the street to where Richter's grocery store had been located. It was also replaced by a heap of debris, concrete, wood, and shattered glass. My *Hauptschule* was not bombed, but my first school, the *Grundschule*, was partially damaged.

Then my Mama and I walked over to one of the apartments that was not destroyed by the bombs and knocked on the door. A middle-aged lady with black hair and glasses whom we did not know greeted us at the door. "*Heil, Hitler*," she said, and her arm went up robotically.

"Do you know where Oskar Roesch is?" asked my Mama, hoping that someone might have seen my grandfather.

"Sorry, I do not know," was the reply. My Mama did not bother to engage her in a conversation about what happened. She came to Chemnitz to see what she could salvage. Once she saw there was nothing left of what we owned, and that she would probably not find my grandparents, my Mama and I went back to Frohburg. We were covered with dust and dirt. When I blew my nose in my handkerchief that night, the handkerchief was black.

We were now living in Frohburg, and a few weeks later my grandparents came to visit us. My grandparents told us what happened that night in Chemnitz. They heard the screaming sirens, and along with everyone else, they started to run across the street into the basement/shelter. My grandmother went ahead and at the last minute, my grandfather tried to take a few things. He grabbed their bedspread and a gravy boat from their china closet. Why he grabbed this, I do not know. They made it to the shelter and waited until they could no longer hear the whirring of the planes in the distance.

Then my grandfather and a few other people went outside. He stood in the park across the street and watched their entire apartment building go up in flames. He saw my Papa's grand piano swallowed up in flames, fall and break through the third floor window and smash to the ground. My Papa had bought that piano when I was around one year old, because he wanted to practice his music on it. I always hoped that one day he would teach me how to play the piano. It cost several months' wages, and we had to pay it off. My Mama had always been upset about it, because there was hardly any money for food and my Papa seemed to not care about that.

As my grandfather stood at the corner and watched, they heard more planes in the distance, and the sirens had gone off again. Everyone ran back into the basement and stayed there until the morning. When they came out the next morning, my grandfather saw that our church, the *Schlosskirche*, had been bombed too. A bomb actually got stuck in the wall of the church and everyone was afraid that it might go off. No one got near the church for a very long time. That church had beautiful stained glass windows and a steeple. Although it was rebuilt after the war, the steeple was not the same, and the beautiful stain-glass windows were eventually replaced by glass windows that were not as pretty.

I do not remember where my grandparents lived right after the bombing. Eventually, they settled in a village in Hetzdorf, a small town in the Erzgebirge section of Saxony. Where they lived for those few weeks after the bombing of Chemnitz, I do not remember.

The war was almost over. Everyone wanted it to be. Towards the end, the government gave each family food stamp rations, but it was never enough. On most days, my Mama sent Renate and me to nearby villages to get food. "Tell the shop owners you will do chores for them in exchange for food," said my Mama.

One day in April, 1945, as Renate and I were walking with our wooden wagon to get food, we thought the sky looked so pretty. There were no clouds. But just as we got past the outskirts of Frohburg and we were walking towards Greifenheim (another small town), we heard sirens and then saw planes in the distance. We frantically looked around for a place to hide. As we were running, we saw bomber planes shooting down a train on the railroad track. We left our wooden wagon in the street and jumped into the indentations on the fields, laid flat, and waited for it to be over. I put my arm across Renate's back to protect her. "Renate, are you OK?" My voice was shaking. Her face was covered with dust, and she had torn her dress.

"Mama will want to fix your dress right away. You only have one more dress," I said to my sister.

"Let's just stay here for a few more minutes in case the planes come back." We stayed in the field arms across each other's back, waiting silently. We heard nothing.

"Do you think it is safe to get up now, Anita?" asked Renate.

"Let's just wait here a few more minutes," I said. I felt so responsible for her.

"Do you think this war is almost over?" asked Renate trembling with fear.

"I hope so, Renate." I said. I started to wonder how long it will be until we see Papa again. I missed him more now than ever.

*****

A few days later, our Mama had no food again. I saw the terror in her eyes. She now had 4 children to feed and did not know from day to day where the food would come from. As the oldest child, I took on much of the feelings of responsibility for the family too. "Anita, go to some of the people in Frohburg, and see if you can trade my mother's table cloth for some potatoes." My Mama was fighting back tears. Erika was crawling on the floor, and Hans was making faces at her. Erika was laughing.

"OK, Mama, I will do that," I said. I gave my Mama a knowing look to try to communicate to her that I would somehow come back with food.

I went from house to house to house with the family wagon. No one wanted the tablecloth. It was one of our few precious possessions and it was so hard for Mama to give it away, yet it seemed to be worthless. I walked all afternoon. There was no way I would come back home without something for our family... So I walked a little farther, to a farmer's home. "Hello, I am Anita Roesch. I live two kilometers (a little over a mile) from here in Frohburg. My family does not have any land, so we can't plant any of our own vegetables. We have 4 children in our family, my father is away in the war and my sister is only a baby. Would you be willing to trade this tablecloth for some potatoes or flour for our family?" I tried to conceal my desperation as I spoke to him. The man whom I spoke with was an older man, a farmer, he was dirty, and looked very tired. I looked right into his dark brown eyes and fought back my own tears of despair.

"Alright, Fraulein, I will give you some potatoes for the tablecloth."

"Thank you so much," I said.

The following week, I had to start all over again. I took my grandmother's curtains and went back to the same farmer. He agreed to trade sugar, flour, and potatoes for the curtains. "Thank you so much. My mother can make soup and really stretch it with the flour. She is a great cook and can make it really good," I said.

*****

I remember when my grandmother in Frohburg told us that the war was over. For one day, there was good news and cause for celebration. My Mama said she was very happy because this meant that the bombing would stop. But people were still so afraid. No one knew what was going to happen next. Our daily life continued to be a struggle. We were just consumed with our survival. Yet for the first few days after it ended, people still robotically put up their arms to greet one another with the "*Heil, Hitler*" and then abruptly and with humiliation put their arms back down and just said "*Gutentag*." When the American troops came into Frohburg, everyone hung white sheets or towels from their windows to let them know they surrendered and would not resist their advances. My Mama hung one of Erika's diapers from my grandmother's apartment window.

A few months after the War ended, I first heard about the Holocaust. I was completely shocked. I felt ashamed. Little by little, crumbs of information were fed to the general population about what actually happened. While we and many others felt victimized by what happened to us in 1945, our eyes were opened as we discovered more about the true nature of the Nazi regime. I just did not want to believe it. "Mama," I said, "How could something like that happen here? I cannot believe it."

"Anita, I cannot believe it either. They lie to us all the time. Look, first they told us Hitler died fighting in Berlin. Then a few days later, we learn that he shot himself in the head," said my Mama.

My Mama continued, “I really cannot even think about it right now. All I worry about is how we are going to eat. I do not know what I would do if I had only young children.” Of course, many Germans were aware of what had been happening, many had taken an active role, some had turned a blind eye, and some were unaware. But it was not until years later, when I was in America, when I saw pictures of the concentration camps that I learned how Jews and others were gassed and burned. The perspective of time helped me begin to understand the extent of the propaganda, manipulation, evil, and cruelty that had characterized the Nazi regime during my childhood.

Even though the American soldiers first arrived in Frohburg, they later moved out, because it was agreed by the Allies that Russian troops would have jurisdiction over the Saxony area of Germany. Because I knew so little of what actually happened in the war, I could not understand why the Russian troops were so angry and revengeful when they arrived in Germany. When they arrived in Germany, they took over homes and dwellings and painted them a screaming bright red or blue.

*****

Next to our grandmother’s apartment, there was a photography studio on Schlossergasse Alley. The photographers had a studio in the back, and they owned the building. The owner’s name was Frau

Kuchen. One day she was not at home, so one of the Russian officers wearing his green uniform came up to our apartment and knocked on the door. “Do you know where Frau Kuchen is? We wanted to use some of the cameras,” he asked.

I stared at him because I could not believe that he wore his shirt over his pants.

“I do not know,” said my Mama.

“What a beautiful child,” said the officer and asked if he could hold Erika. “She looks like my daughter.” The tall Russian officer picked Erika up and said some words in Russian.

“Thank you, Frau Roesch. Please let Frau Kuchen know that I was looking for her.”

“*Jawohl*,” said my Mama. A day after he left, we realized that we had all gotten lice. My Mama put gasoline, or something that smelled like it, on all our heads. I don’t know where she got whatever it was, but it killed the lice.

*****

Two months after the war ended, I went to Chemnitz. I do not remember why I needed to go there. But I do remember that I got off at the wrong stop because I could not find or recognize any of the landmarks. I could not find the *Rathaus* (City Hall). The city was nothing but partially destroyed buildings. The city was under ashes that looked like we had a snowfall that was two feet deep. It made an impression on me I have never forgotten. I grew up in this town, I knew it as well as I knew my own house and now I could not even recognize where I was. One thing I realized is that the wounds of war may heal, but there will always be a scar and things can never be the same as they were before.

During the summer right after the war, in 1945, Renate and I (who were now 10 and 13) somehow managed to convince some farmers in Nenkersdorf to let us do chores for them in exchange for food. Nenkersdorf was about two kilometers (a little over a mile) from Frohburg, so we could walk there. They had a big farm. We spent our days picking strawberries, peeling potatoes, and doing whatever else they needed us to do. In exchange, they gave us potatoes and flour that we could bring home to our Mama. After a few weeks, I asked them to hire my Mama, too. They agreed. So, once or twice a week, my Mama put one-year-old Erika in the wagon, and Hans walked along with her. She did their wash and other light chores in exchange for potatoes, vegetables, flour, and cheese.

One time, when Renate and I were in Nenkersdorf, Frau Kaufmann's cook asked us if we wanted to eat some dumplings. She had just made them.

"Oh, yes," Renate and I both said in unison.

"Girls, why don't you see which one of you can eat the most?" asked Frau Kaufmann. I thought she was joking, but she must have known how hungry we were, and it was a sensitive way to let us eat as much as we could. I don't remember who won the contest, but

I remember that we ate 15 dumplings between the two of us. Herr and Frau Kaufmann helped us so much that summer. Later, when East Germany was formed, they had to give up their farm and turn it over to the government. They were stunned, angry and full of disbelief. This farm was their property and had been in their family for three generations. How could the government just take it? They didn't even pay them for the land. As I watched all of this, I started to wonder if communism was going to be any better than Hitler...

After the war ended, it took several months for schools to open and businesses to start functioning again and even longer until reliable transportation was once again established. Once I was back in school by that fall, I offered to do other students' homework in exchange for flour or potatoes. Sometimes I did four or five different stories on the same subject just to get food from the other students, those students who had farms or even some land and could plant their own vegetables.

*****

On Palm Sunday, one year after the war ended, my school friends and I were confirmed at Saint Michaelis Church in Frohburg. All of us were so excited. My Mama's sister, Tante Hilde, made my black dress. All the girls wore black at that time. The boys wore dark suits. Confirmation is a reaffirmation of the Christian faith that was taught by one's parents. I always wanted to learn more about God, in fact, I was really searching for God. Somehow, I felt that I was missing something. There had to be more to this Christian experience, I thought.

We each received a confirmation verse from the Bible. My Bible verse was 1 John 2:17:

"The world and its desires will pass away,
but the man who does the will of God lives forever."

The verse did not make any sense to me and I did not think very much about it after that day.

*****

In 1947, at the age of 15, I got a job at Schmidt's deli in Frohburg, a short walk each day from my home. The owners had a small store front, and they lived upstairs. At this time, the government rationed potatoes for a family for the entire winter. My job was to shovel the potatoes onto a cart, weigh them, and give them to the people in exchange for their ration card. Then I took my employer's large wooden wagon and got cheese and milk from the local farmers. Often the farmers gave me extra cheese or flour, which I could drop off at my Mama's place on my way back to the deli. Later, I lived with my employers at the deli during the week and went to school only on Saturdays. The money I earned plus any extra food that my employers or the farmers gave me was walked back to my Mama each weekend.

Finally, more than two years after the war ended, my Papa returned home in the summer of 1947. We didn't know where he was or what happened to him. We learned later that he spent two years in a POW camp. By the time he returned, our family had been without our Papa for five years. He seldom spoke of his war experiences. The only thing I remember is that he was originally assigned to do Morse code, but when he heard any kind of music, he could not concentrate on the Morse code. So they moved him over to work the telephones.

We were just glad he was back home. Our family had no warning about his coming. I was actually the first to see him. I was walking towards the library in Frohburg while he was walking back to Frohburg from the train station. We met each other on the street, and he said to me, "*Bist Du die Roesch Anita*?" ["Are you Anita Roesch?"] His mouth did not smile, but his eyes were sparkling and wet. I immediately hugged him and he me. He looked exactly the same to me. He thought it was me, but since it had been several years, he just wanted to make sure first. I guess I no longer looked like the 12 year old daughter he last saw.

Then we walked to the apartment together and he saw Erika for the first time. Erika was now almost three years old. My Mama and Erika lived in the apartment since my grandmother had died. Renate, Hans, and I continued to sleep at different people's apartments.

We were glad to have our Papa back home. Erika did not go to him for a long time. She just clung to my Mama. This naturally hurt my Papa since he was so eager to reconnect with his family and get to know his new daughter. After he came home, he eventually started a band, and he also conducted the *Frohburger Feuerwehr Kappelle* (Frohburg Fire Company Band). They usually performed at the *Gruene Aue*, a restaurant and dance hall in Frohburg. He sometimes played at the *Frohburg Schuetzenhaus*, where Heinz and I took our dance classes. At the end of each night, whether they played in a hall or in a restaurant, my Papa divided the earnings evenly among his band members. When it came time to pay the taxes, my earnings from my job at the construction materials company helped to cover those taxes.

One day, my Papa came home from Chemnitz after playing with his band.

"*Grosse*, I heard that Herr Zimmerman died of starvation. Someone found him in his apartment." I heard the words, but I could not believe that had happened to my former teacher. I went numb. "No, that is not possible," I said.

*****

Two years later, in 1949, East Germany was officially formed. It became part of the Eastern block of Eastern European nations that were aligned with the Soviet Union. The transition to Communism happened quickly. I had a friend who owned a nursery in Frohburg, where she sold beautiful plants and flowers. In 1949, her business along with all the others were taken over the by East German/ Russian government. She became an employee of the state, no longer a business owner, which greatly troubled her. Her mother had built the business from the ground up and they were very proud of the success they enjoyed. She and her mother had the gift of putting beautiful bouquets of flowers together. My friend knew she had no choice in the matter, so she just accepted it on the outside. Even though we never talked about it, I saw a change in her countenance; she no longer had the light and joy in her eyes that seemed to spark her creativity. The changes were confusing to all of us. As we were trying to process them, they continued at an even greater pace.

Soon after, East German police and Russian troops came to our apartment and told us to vote. When I got to city hall, I said to Renate, "This is silly. They tell you to come out and vote, and then there is only one name on the ballot anyway." We were given a piece of paper, told to fold it up, and gave it back. A government official took note of our attendance.

A few days later, my Papa looked uneasy as he sat across from me at our kitchen table. "*Grosse*, you can't talk like that about the voting. Someone overheard you, and they came here and said there would be trouble for you if you ever spoke up like that again. Just don't say anything about it anymore," he warned. I remembered the sign that I read a few years earlier about how the enemy is always listening. I realized then that in East Germany, it was not going to be much better than Nazism. People were still afraid. I just wanted to be free to be myself, but I silently submitted to what was expected and required.

*****

"For a man's ways are in full view of the Lord, and he examines all his paths." Proverbs 5:21

—4—

Working and Waiting in West Germany

As soon as Frau Fischer and I crossed over the bridge into the French sector of Berlin, I was immediately struck by the differences between the two Germanys. It was like looking at black-and-white pictures in East Germany and color pictures in West Germany. The West German roads were busy, and people were bustling and walking around everywhere. Stores were crowded. There were many things to buy, a lot of variety and colors. People in West Germany seemed to have nicer clothes. Their shoes seemed stylish and new. Homes had been rebuilt with quality building materials and painted with bright colors. I saw all this as I walked and took it all in.

Frau Fischer walked me to Frau Schiller's apartment and introduced us. Frau Schiller was a typical German Frau. Her small apartment was immaculate—not a crumb on the floor. Her apartment was on one floor with a small kitchen, one bedroom, and one bathroom. I noticed that the home was relatively empty—there were no pictures of family, no decorations; it was just clean and open. Frau Schiller was a widow: her husband had been killed in the war. She wouldn't talk about what happened to him. Only Frau Schiller knew how he died, and Frau Schiller never told anyone (at least to my knowledge).

When I first walked in, I thought she was very timid. She seemed to jump when someone began to talk. She had gray hair and round glasses that were too big for her face. Although she was only 68, she had so many wrinkles on her face; I thought she looked about 80. But her energy level reflected that of a 40-year-old, and she was also quite thin. She immediately fussed about what Frau Fischer and I would eat and spoke to me in the familiar "*du*" ("you"), which put me at ease. Germans never use the familiar except among family members and very close friends. Her choice to use "*du*" with me was extremely kind. She insisted that I address her in the familiar "*du*" as well. She must have sensed how drained I was from the day, and she was very welcoming.

Since it was lunch time, "Please sit down, Anita. Do you want something to eat?" she asked, as she started to put on a white tablecloth and set coffee cups and saucers on her square wooden table.

I didn't want anything to eat. But I sat at the kitchen table with them and talked a while until it was almost dinner time. I cannot recall one thing that we talked about the entire day. My mind kept racing ahead to tomorrow. Will I really be able to get to West Germany? While it was a relief to be out of East Germany, I still felt like I had to keep looking over my shoulder. I had not yet reached safety. When I wasn't imagining scenarios about tomorrow, I was imagining what was my family doing? What were they thinking? Will they be OK? Will I ever see them again?

"Anita, my sister-in-law will walk you to the airport tomorrow. She will take care of everything," said the ever-confident Frau Fischer.

After that, Frau Fischer went back to East Berlin on the Underground, and I spent the night with Frau Schiller.

Frau Schiller offered me a thin nightgown and gave me sheets to sleep on the sofa. I guessed she was often lonely, since she wanted to keep talking about all kinds of things—the division of Germany, the economy, and how bad it was for the East Germans.

"Anita, it is so terrible for the East Germans. Even if they work hard, they cannot buy anything of good quality anyway. They cannot even buy good clothes," she said.

"You did the right thing, Anita. You will not regret your decisions," she continued.

After a while, my mind wandered, and I thought of my family. I finally admitted I wanted to get some rest, so Frau Schiller retired to the bedroom, and I spread out her sheets on the sofa. As I lay there, I heard the cars driving by, the wind blowing, and Frau Schiller's furnace whirring. Every sound was unfamiliar and louder than what I was used to. I tossed on the sofa all night and thought only of my family. I wondered if my Mama would be OK. I kept looking at the clock—2 AM, I wondered if I would ever see her again. I hoped that I would be able to see my Mama again, maybe while I was in West Germany. 3 AM, will Karli even remember me? He was so much fun. I was almost a second mother to him. I felt so guilty about leaving him behind. 4 AM: did Renate get back home OK? I hoped she went right to Mama in Frohburg to let her know that Frau Fischer and Frau Schiller were doing all they could to help me. 5:12 AM: I hope my father will understand why I left. Why couldn't I just fall asleep? It felt like torture to me and was even more frightening than when the bombs were dropping. I knew the next few days would be hard, so sleep would have been good. 5:16AM was the last time I saw the clock. From sheer exhaustion, my mind finally allowed my body to sleep.

I was still trembling a little that morning. Frau Schiller came out of her bedroom and sat next to me on the sofa. She was still wearing her nightgown and robe. Sensing my emotions, Frau Schiller thought to ask me about Heinz. "Well Anita, tell me about this wonderful man that you are going to marry. What is his profession?" So that morning, I explained to Frau Schiller how Heinz and I had met and how he got to America after working in West Germany for four years.

"Anita, that is so wonderful that Heinz wants to marry you. You have your whole life ahead of you. How many children do you want to have?"

"Oh, I hope to have at least three or four children," I said with a slight laugh. "My little brother Karli is only five. I wonder if he will even remember me." I thought and said aloud.

Frau Schiller then gently changed the subject. "Anita, did you tell anyone at your job at the factory about what you were planning to do?" she asked, very carefully.

"No, Frau Schiller. I could not take a chance that someone might turn me in. I did not say anything to anyone. I guess they will realize that I am missing today and eventually try and get in touch with my Mama. I suppose my Mama will just tell them the truth—that I left East Germany for good." I was then gripped with fear that my Mama might have to go through some great difficulty because of what I was doing.

After we finished talking, I did take a bath. Frau Schiller got the bath water ready and put out a towel and a wash cloth and some soap. Although I had used her bathroom when we first arrived, that morning I noticed the white, soft toilet paper she had. The toilet paper in East Germany was grayish, almost like crepe paper, but thicker, and rough. Yet another stark difference between the two Germanys.

While I bathed, Frau Schiller started making breakfast—German sausages, toast with butter and jelly, and rolls. And she brewed some coffee. Lathering up the soap and letting the water pour over every inch of my body, I felt the stress washing away. The warm water relaxed me. For a moment, I felt frozen in time. I did not want to escape the safety of the warm water in the tub. Yet I could smell the food while I bathed, and I was hungry. Frau Schiller had everything ready for me at the kitchen table. Once I was dressed, she warmly welcomed and directed me over to her table. I put on the heavy blue dress; the one Renate had worn the day before. I remember being overwhelmed at Frau Schiller's kindness. She had never even met me before.

Although I was conflicted with many fears, I was still resolved to continue down the path I was on. Deep down inside, I recognized that I was doing what was right for me. I knew I had to leave West Berlin by plane and fly to Frankfurt, West Germany. Heinz had friends in a very small town in West Germany, a train ride from Frankfurt, and he had left a little bit of money for me there. I had not really planned about the money. If Frau Schiller had not offered to give me the money for the plane and for the train once I got to Frankfurt, I would have had to find a job somewhere in West Berlin until I had earned enough to fly out. I was glad I didn't have to find a job in West Berlin because I thought it would be too easy for the East German police to find me. This woman, who was a complete stranger to me less than 24 hours ago, gave me a lifeline and hope through her incredible generosity.

Frau Schiller also offered to give me extra money for the train fare so I could go directly from Frankfurt to Oberhausen-Osterfeld, the town in West Germany where Heinz's friend lived. Heinz had worked in the coalmines in Oberhausen-Osterfeld before he left for

America. Since Frau Schiller was willing to lend me the money, I could keep moving. I promised to pay her back as soon as I could find work in West Germany. She then asked me more questions about Heinz.

"Where are Heinz's parents?" she asked. Her genuine interest in Heinz and in me was like someone wrapping a warm blanket across my body.

"Oh, they are still in East Germany, in Frohburg, where my parents live," I said. My words and mind were beginning to separate—I answered her questions, but I began to think of the fear I was feeling. After we finished eating and as Frau Schiller began to clear the breakfast dishes, she talked about the best way to get to Tempelhof airport in Berlin. My emotional pendulum had swung from the conversation about Heinz to sorrow and guilt about leaving my Mama again. I choked up and said very little as Frau Schiller reasoned aloud about the best way for me to go.

"Anita, I think it would be best if I walk to the airport with you. I can wait with you until you get a plane for Frankfurt. If you want me to, I can send a letter to your Mama so she will know that you got on the airplane," she said. That meant so much to me. I was so overwhelmed and yet so grateful that Frau Schiller was thinking clearly. We packed up my belongings. Frau Schiller offered to give me some of her soap and shampoo, a toothbrush and some toothpaste. We packed those items into the bag, and then Frau Schiller directed me to her door.

Neither of us said very much as we walked to the airport. I do not remember if we also needed to take a trolley to get there. It was another cold day. When we arrived at the airport, Frau Schiller bought the one-way ticket. The flight was scheduled for 1PM. We had some time, so we sat down in a waiting area. Frau Schiller had brought along some butter sandwiches. I was nervous again, but I forced them down. I could not even imagine what I would be doing the next day.

Frau Schiller waited with me until the flight was ready to board. No one checked for ID or questioned where I was going or why. A wave of relief came over me. What I didn't realize was that, at the time, many East Germans were leaving this way, and the West German officials did not ask any questions. In fact, West Germany granted any East German citizen asylum and citizenship in the country. The West German people and officials were very helpful. Just before I boarded the plane, I asked Frau Schiller to write down her address so that I could repay her once I started working. She pulled out a piece of paper from her purse and wrote it down for me. At that point, I welled up again. I just felt so alone. I did not know where I was going. I felt so vulnerable. Frau Schiller put her arms around me and said, "Anita you have your entire life ahead of you. You are a good person. I know you will find happiness with Heinz and in America. I will send that letter to your Mama tonight, so she will not be worrying. She will know that you made it to Frankfurt at least."

"Frau Schiller, thank you so much," I managed to say. Tears filled with gratitude and relief moved down my cheeks. We waved goodbye, and I followed the other passengers and boarded the plane. At the time, I was in such a daze and desperately needed Frau Schiller for this next step. It's hard to believe that less than 24 hours earlier, she had no idea I what I was planning to do, she had not seen me in a long time and yet, she embraced me, and took on my challenge as her own. Her generosity was exorbitant and I was left wondering, "Why would she do all of this for me? Why would she take the risk? Why would she be so generous and trust me with her money at a time when no one had enough even for their own needs?"

Once I found my seat, I realized that the plane was completely full. The plane took off immediately and I tried to settle into my seat. As I listened to some of the conversations, I realized that many people had left East Germany as I had. They lied to the guards somehow. The young man seated behind me was talking to a young woman next to him and said, "I lied to the guard and told him that I had to go to a funeral for my grandmother in West Berlin. Now I am going to look for a job in West Germany. I hope to get my younger brother out, too." I also overheard two young men across from me talking of meeting up with contacts in Frankfurt in the hopes of finding a job. The people in front me had relatives in West Germany and talked about what they knew of the differences between the two Germanys. "For one thing, you can buy food whenever you want to. It is not rationed, and the food is of very good quality." Hearing all of these stories somehow strengthened me for the lonely journey ahead.

As I sat on the plane, I hoped my apprehension would be lost in the clouds. If I had not been so tense, I might have enjoyed the adventure. But I didn't see it that way. I was still clutched by fear.

I was on the plane for about two hours. I threw up the entire time, as did another man sitting near me. I held my bag tightly in my fists, always ready in case I had to open it up. Since I had never been on a plane before, I wasn't sure if I was sick from my nerves or from the motion. When the plane finally landed, I was so thankful. As I walked off the plane into the Frankfurt airport, I had no idea where to go. I knew that Heinz's friends in Oberhausen-Osterfeld were at least a three-hour train ride away.

It was still afternoon, and I do not remember how I got to the train station or if it was within walking distance from the airport in Frankfurt, but somehow, I was able to get on a train that afternoon for Oberhausen-Osterfeld. Emotions were dominating my mind, and I just kept moving on almost robotically. I do not remember anything about my arrival or if I walked to Heinz's friend's apartment, but I do remember that I arrived there by that same evening.

Osterfeld is a small village near a larger town, Oberhausen, in West Germany. The largest nearby city is Dusseldorf. I never knew why Heinz ended up in this town or how he met Helmut. But Heinz assured me in his letters that Helmut would help me once I arrived.

Although Heinz worked at various jobs in West Germany, Osterfeld was his last stop before he embraced his dream, America.

Helmut's little apartment building was one of many in the small town of Osterfeld. Osterfeld was actually a small pretty little town, compared to Oberhausen, which was all concrete, like a city, with very little green to look at. In this part of West Germany, the landscape was flat. Even though it was in December when I arrived, I could see that blueberry bushes covered one side of Helmut's apartment building like a blanket, though it was still a long time before the berries would come out and be ripe for picking. Commanding trees with huge bare branches were spread throughout the front and back yards of the apartment buildings. When I knocked, I was uncomfortable again because I would be at the mercy of another unfamiliar person. My journey to America was like this, the path ahead of me was not always visible, and I had to learn to trust complete strangers not only to realize my dream, but for my survival and safety. That wonderful safe nest of my loving family was behind me now, and I was truly alone. Helmut answered the door and recognized me, although we never met before.

"Anita," he exclaimed, in a deep, loud, guttural German voice. He looked like a country man, with large red cheeks, a black mustache and beard, and a large gut. He was only in his early 30s, but he looked middle-aged.

"How did you know it was me?" I asked.

"Oh, Heinz showed me your picture, and he recently wrote telling me that you might be coming soon."

"Please come in, *Bitte*," said Helmut. He used the familiar '*Du*' form of "you" when speaking with me that put me at ease. In Germany, this usage is reserved for close friends and family. Here was another person who I never met before embracing me and welcoming me in to his circle of family and friends. He waved me into his home and immediately called to his wife Christl to come and meet me. Christl was a very attractive woman with blue eyes, blonde hair, and a very red complexion as well. She was also 8 months' pregnant with their first child, and she seemed very uncomfortable as she walked very slowly towards the door. I immediately felt like I was imposing on them.

Helmut invited me to sit down with them in their living room.

"So how was it getting here, Anita? Did you have any trouble getting out of East Germany?" he asked.

"Well, actually, a friend helped me cross the bridge," I answered.

"You can stay with us for as long as you need to, Anita," Helmut said as he motioned for Christl to sit down as well. As I looked at Christl, I could see that she was very uneasy, and the last thing she needed was to be taking care of someone else. Helmut offered to let me stay in the room that was already ready-made for the baby. He had a cot that he could roll into that room until I was ready to be on my own. We walked over to it, and I could see the baby's room was already set up with a large wooden crib. Some baby clothes were folded in a pile on a small table. Christl had painted the walls with blue clouds.

I spent the evening with them and ate dinner there. The meal was good: bratwurst, sauerkraut, and *brot* (bread). Helmut drank his dark German beer. I had some coffee. Christl drank *apfelsaft* (apple juice): she explained she was doing her best to eat right for the baby.

After dinner, I felt really guilty about imposing on them, but I had no choice but to stay there. Helmut's mother came by later that evening and I realized that she also lived with them. She was a very nice lady; she was tall and soft spoken. Helmut later remembered that Heinz had left some West German deutschmarks for me. It was enough money to buy a few outfits and some food for a little while. I was relieved when he handed me the envelope me because I really did not want to ask for it and didn't really know how to bring it up. The envelope had my name written on it. It was in Heinz's handwriting.

That night, I was so tired; I had no trouble falling asleep. I had traveled far in those past two days, yet the steps were bittersweet. Although the geographical distance between Frohburg and Oberhausen was only 500 kilometers (about 300 miles), I had almost gone in a circle to get there, so the actual distance that I traveled was much farther. I felt like I grew up and aged 5 years through my experiences that had started less than 48 hours ago.

The next morning, I asked Christl if I could leave my small bag while I went to look for a job. Helmut did not have a car, but he did offer to walk with me. From the living room, I heard Helmut tell Christl to get breakfast ready. When I sat down at their kitchen table, I noticed that Christl had made coffee and cakes for breakfast and the table was already set. The coffee smelled so good and it warmed me from the inside and out. I took a bath and got ready. As I looked in the small mirror that hung on their bathroom wall, I thought I looked so tired. Could those be a few gray hairs that I saw for the first time? I looked so pale. I was very sad again that morning thinking of my family and all that was precious to me that I left behind, yet I was very motivated to find work.

I decided that I would just take whatever job I could find, it did not matter. I just needed to earn enough money for my living expenses and to pay Frau Schiller back. Before I left, I asked Christl for some paper and an envelope and I wrote to my Mama.

"*Meine liebe gute Mama* (my dear good Mama), I made it safely to Oberhausen-Osterfeld. I am staying with Heinz's friends. Do not worry about me. I will write you again when I have found a job." It made me relax a little to know that these few lines would mean so much to my Mama and would be like a gift to her.

I smiled and turned to wave as I headed down the hill towards the main part of town. I had no plan except to find work and a permanent place to stay. The money that Heinz had left for me was not going to last very long, so I was worried.

When I got to the main street in Oberhausen, I saw a hospital named *Elizabeth Krankenhaus* (Elizabeth Hospital). I thought they might need employees, so I decided to walk in, and I asked to speak to the hospital administrator. It was a large multi-story hospital, and I reasoned it must be in the very center of the town. The town itself was not very pretty. There were hardly any trees, just building after building. Some were stores and others must have been office buildings. A young nun escorted me into an office and told to wait about 15 minutes. It was obviously a Catholic hospital, because many of the nurses and employees were nuns. I sat in a chair across from the administrator's desk and noticed a large wooden crucifix on the wall behind her desk. The administrator also had a glass candy jar on the end of the desk with some type of candy in it. I do not remember any more than that.

When *Oberschwester* (Head nun) Hildegard Bauer finally came in, I stood up, shook hands, and introduced myself. "Please sit down, Fraulein," she insisted. She had a kind round face and blue eyes, but very yellow teeth. I guessed her to be in her mid-30s. She was slim and tall. She wore the dark black nun outfit, and her head was also covered. She also had dark-rimmed glasses that made her look very intelligent. I then told her my story: how I defected from East Germany and wanted to work in West Germany to establish myself. I didn't bother to tell her about the plan to go to America. I needed a job, and it would take at least a year to get the permission to go to America. Oberschwester Hildegard nodded with respect and understanding as I went through the whole story. After I finished, I simply said that I would be willing to do any job that was available and if she knew of a place to stay, too, that would be even better. I figured I had nothing to lose at this point. I could tell she liked me.

"Did you finish high school, Fraulein?"

It was a fair question, since many young people never finished school during the war. Once the schools were closed, many never went back because they needed to work. "Yes, I finished high school. I did it on Saturdays while I worked for a delicatessen in my hometown,"

"Did you want to study at the university?" she asked.

"I wanted to, but there was no opportunity for me. I started working to help my Mama. Then I later learned to do quality control testing for a company that I worked for. I studied for a year. There were only three people in East Germany who had passed the test, and I was one of them," I answered with surprising confidence.

"How did you get into this?" she asked.

"I was working in the factory, and my boss asked me if I wanted to become a *Werkstoffpruefer* (quality control tester). I figured, why not?"

She seemed to be taking some notes.

"Is your family all still in East Germany?" she asked and looked right into my eyes.

"Yes, they are," I said.

"Well, then, why did you leave?" she asked.

I could not decide whether to tell her about Heinz. I did not want her to think that I would leave the job right away. But I am no good at lying, so I just answered her.

"My fiancé was also from Frohburg. He worked in West Germany for four years before coming to America. I hope to work for a year or two and then go to America also." The Oberschwester looked down at her papers and just smiled.

"Fraulein," she explained, "we have to do everything by the book. All your papers have to be in order. You have to go to the officials in Oberhausen city hall and give up your East German identification card. They will automatically accept you as a West German citizen and issue you a new West German passport. Once you have done that, come back here and I will find a job that you can do at this hospital. Also, there are about 20 women who live in rooms, about four women to a room, on the top floor of this hospital, also employees. You can stay there, too, if you like."

I didn't know what to say. It was too good to believe. It just seemed like journey had already been planned by someone and everything was in place and ready when I arrived. There are so many people in West Germany who did not have jobs; how could I have been so fortunate to get a job and a place to live on my very first day in the country? I couldn't wait, and so I went right from the hospital to City Hall and took care of the papers. I felt guilty and relieved all at the same time as I surrendered my East German passport. They asked me if I or my parents had been in the Nazi party. "No, we were not in the Nazi party," I answered. I wondered why that was being asked, now ten years after the war. But it was necessary, and I did what was necessary. I walked back to the hospital administrator's office and presented her with my papers. I barely noticed the beautiful day.

When I came back, Oberschwester Hildegard invited me back to her office.

"*Gut*," she said, "then, *Fraulein,* you have a job and can start tomorrow. Your job will be to do the laundry/ linens in the hospital. You can live on the floor with the other women that do this type of work. Hospital meals are also included as part of your compensation."

I was just thrilled. Knowing that I had a place to live and food prepared for me each day was more than I could have hoped for. "And," said Oberschwester Hildegard, "this is a Catholic hospital, so I expect your behavior to be above reproach. The work is hard, but I have a feeling you will be able to handle it. See you tomorrow, then."

The next morning, I said good-bye to Helmut and Christl and thanked them for everything. I was thrilled that I did not need to depend on them anymore. I knew they were excited about the arrival of their baby. I would have been an imposition if I had stayed. So I moved into the living space on the top floor of the hospital and started working. I shared a hospital room with three other women. We each had our own bed. There was a small window in our room. One bathroom down the hall was shared by all 20 of us. I was thankful just to have plumbing, hot water, a job, and food. That night, I wrote letters to my Mama first and then to Heinz. I knew my Mama would be so happy that I had a place to live.

The next day, I washed one of my three dresses and slip and hung it on a line outside of our living quarters. I went to the cafeteria to get something to eat, and when I came back to get my clothes from the line, they were gone. One of the other employees must have stolen them, but I could not imagine who would have done it. I never asked anyone if they knew what happened. After that, I had only two dresses, and I had to keep washing them over and over again.

I became friendly with the twenty women or so that lived with me there at the hospital. They were all very nice. Most were young girls in their late teens or early twenties like me. A few were older, in their 40s. Some had lost their fathers and brothers in the war. One woman's story was particularly shocking and upsetting to me. Brigitte lived in Berlin in 1945 and spoke of being repeatedly raped by the Russian soldiers. After they raped her, they raped her fourteen-year-old daughter. Her daughter was married now and seemed to be OK, but Brigitte said she herself would never get over it. I had heard rumors about rapes, but I didn't know of anyone until I met Brigitte. With all of the hardship my family suffered, at least none of us had to experience the terrible trauma of rape.

The nun in charge of the laundry and I worked really well together. I worked hard and never complained. Since I did not know anyone in the town, I would often keep working even after my shift was over just to help the nuns who were in charge. My job entailed washing the sheets and folding and stacking them in the storage room. We also washed the nuns' clothes, their underwear, and the doctors' shirts. I had never used an iron before. We worked about 10 hours each day. We got one day off every fourteen days. Many of the other hospital employees were also nuns. Because the women who worked there had come from all different parts of Germany with different German dialects, we all had to speak High German so that we could understand each other.

I was very impressed with the nuns. They worked hard, and they believed their service was for God. The nuns who were nurses really wanted to show God's love to their sick patients. They prayed with patients and offered them hope and friendship. I thought it was admirable, but I did not understand why they would want to give their whole lives to this kind of work and not get married and have families of their own. I wanted to believe in God, but to me He was distant. I just worked hard and tried my best to get along with everyone. That strategy seemed to work well for me.

Sometimes I went back to visit Helmut and his family. As I got to know his mother, I learned that she was a very strong believer in Christ. She gave me a copy of the Psalms and New Testament and showed me verses that I should read and use as a guide. I respected her and saw that her faith was real in her life and that she did her best to live by the Bible. Here are some of the verses she suggested that I read:

- Psalm 121:7, 'The Lord will keep you from all harm—he will watch over your life.'
- Psalm 55:23, 'But you, O God, will bring down the wicked into the pit of corruption; bloodthirsty and deceitful men will not live out half their days.'
- Psalm 37:5, 'Commit your way to the Lord; trust in him and he will do this.'
- John 16:23, 'in that day you will no longer ask me anything. I tell you the truth, my Father will give you whatever you ask in my name.'

I still have the small piece of paper with her handwriting on it, tucked securely in the tiny Bible that she gave me. She often read the Bible with me and prayed for me and my family. I was grateful for her concern and her willingness to do what she could for me. But to me, God was distant. Sometimes I tried to read the Bible, but I didn't seem to comprehend why people like Helmut's mother got so much from it. I didn't see much of God in Germany during the war and not much after the war either. Was God really alive and active in our world or was the Bible just a collection of myths and stories from the past? I just did not know; however, I thanked Helmut's mother and something just made me want to keep that piece of paper. Maybe I would understand later?

After I had lived in West Germany for about six months, I bought another pair of shoes and one more outfit with my earnings. I had paid Frau Schiller back with those first few weeks of earnings. I wrote to my Mama and to Heinz two times a week. Heinz wrote to me all the time, too. In his letters, Heinz often told me how many days he had left until he would be finished with the army. Heinz had joined the army as soon as he arrived in America because immigrants would receive instant citizenship if they enlisted in the army. He thought this was the best plan to pave the way for me since I would be a legal immigrant because I was coming to the US to marry a US citizen. He served in the American army during the Korean War; however, he was never deployed to Korea because his understanding of English was so limited. Instead, he was given work at an Army base in Georgia, where he provided maintenance services and also built furniture for some of the commanding officers since he was a highly skilled cabinet maker.

In his letters, Heinz wrote about his uncles and how kind they had been to him. He often mentioned how welcomed he felt when he first got to America because his Uncle Wilhelm (the man who had sponsored him) and his Uncle Fritz were so nice to him. He was always invited there for holidays and birthdays. It made the separation from his own father and family a lot easier for him.

In his last letter, Heinz told me that he had two weeks leave from the army and that he was going to fly to West Germany to see if we could marry in Germany. I was so excited at the thought of seeing him again—it had been five years! By the time I got the letter from Heinz, I had only two weeks to prepare. I had been working on getting the needed paperwork, but I was unsure that I would have everything on time. Either way, I thought it was so wonderful that he was flying to West Germany to see me. Heinz invited our mothers, my Mama and Marta, to join us in Oberhausen.

In the meantime, I wrote to and reminded my Mama that I needed copies of my birth certificate and any other papers that would help identify me.

It was June of 1956 when Heinz arrived in West Germany, and I was so excited. He surprised me by showing up at the hospital and waiting for my shift to end. The nuns kept talking about this handsome man who was waiting in the cafeteria. Oberschwester Hildegard found me and told me I could finish early that day and that I had someone waiting there. When I walked into the cafeteria, I was completely overcome with happiness. I am sure my heart stopped beating for a bit. I knew Heinz was coming, but I had no idea it would be that day. We hugged, kissed, and cried, while I tried to tell him all that had happened. He tried to tell me about the papers we needed to get married. The Oberschwester was kind enough to give me a leave of absence for those two weeks—I would have never asked for the time off—but she was a sensitive person, and I really appreciated her kindness.

Our mothers arrived in Oberhausen two days after Heinz did. Seeing Heinz and now seeing my Mama again was such a comfort to me. I never thought I would see her again so soon. We went to Oberhausen City Hall to apply for a marriage license, but we needed permissions from both governments. They explained that we would not get the permissions in time since the correspondence would take more than the two weeks. We were more than disappointed. It would have been so nice to have our mothers as witnesses. Yet, we made the best of it by enjoying the time with them. Heinz took us shopping, and we bought plain gold rings that served as our engagement and wedding bands. So at least we were officially engaged.

We made the most of the time with our mothers. Heinz took us out to dinner and we walked around the town. I spent most of the time talking to my Mama. "How is Papa? How about Renate, Erika, Hans, and Karli?" I wanted to know everything that they were doing. I missed them all so much. Heinz wanted to buy something for our mothers, too, so he suggested they each pick out a blouse and he would pay for it. After a few days, they returned to East Germany. Saying good-bye was very difficult. I was sad all over again. "Well, Anita," said Heinz, "we will make our own family in America, we will have lots of children. It shouldn't be long now, Anita, for all the paperwork to go through." I wonder how Heinz felt when so much of my conversation was about how much I missed my family. He never said a word about it.

We marveled at how West Germany was prospering. Oranges, bananas, and good chocolate were readily available. We felt guilty that some people in East Germany could not even buy deodorant or toothpaste all the time. "There is always plenty to buy in West Germany," I said to Heinz.

"Wait until you get to America," Heinz said. "There is plenty to buy there, too. You won't have to worry about that!" Heinz laughed when he said that. The size of America was just something I could never grasp until I actually got there.

I still thought of my family. Many people in East Germany did not have indoor plumbing, including Heinz's parents. In East Germany, you might be able to buy certain clothes one day, but then those items would not be in the stores again for a few weeks. If you wanted to fix up your apartment, there was no paint for sale in East Germany. But in West Germany, one could buy all kinds of paints, with many color options. Even the items produced in East Germany could not be purchased there. The Erzgebirge, in Saxony where I was from, was famous for making hand-made wooden crafts (then and now). Items like wooden tree ornaments, nutcrackers, and all beautiful handmade art were exported. But if East Germans themselves were able to buy any of it at all, they could buy only the defective ones—and even they were always in limited supply.

Almost everyone in West Germany seemed to have some kind of job; that was not true of the East Germans. The West Germans seemed to be content, while the East Germans were not. Heinz laughed as I talked about all the contrasts I had noticed. He knew I understood that we were doing the right thing and that meant a lot to him.

When Heinz left Germany, he told me not to worry: "Ach, Anita, the worst is behind you now. All you have to do is wait for the approval from the West German government to come to America. Once you get there, we can get married right away." I was excited about going to America. To me, it was "untouchable": no one would ever start a war there. I wanted to raise a family in a safe place.

After Heinz left, I continued the process of applying for a visa to go to America. I had the required sponsor, Heinz's uncle Fritz, and my birth certificate and West German passport. During one interview, I was asked, "Were you ever in the Nazi party?" I could not believe that I was being asked this question again. "No, I was never in the Nazi party, nor were my parents." "What did your father do for a living?" was the next question. "Where are your parents now?" I answered all the questions and hoped for a quick reply.

Also after Heinz left, I sent some West German food—some of the expensive chocolate and some oranges—to my Mama. Heinz had left some extra West German marks that he didn't use. Years later, I found out that the oranges were moldy by the time they arrived, but in her letter back to me, my Mama only thanked me for them.

When I realized we were having so much trouble getting the permissions from both governments for us to get married, I began to think about what I might do if the permissions were not granted for me to immigrate to America. Heinz was now a U.S. citizen, and he would never come back to Europe. As I thought about it, I knew Oberhausen was not where I planned to stay for the rest of my life. If the worst news was to come and I would not get the permissions, I had decided that I would leave West Germany and move to Switzerland. Switzerland was always neutral in wars. It was the next best thing to being in America because it was free from possible future wars.

Heinz continued to help me with the process. He was anxious for me to get the permissions. This letter arrived a month after his visit to West Germany:

> 17.7.56
>
> My dear Anita,
>
> I sent all the papers in this letter. Please send them to Frankfurt. I will explain everything to you. The birth certificate, you had it translated three times in English. One of these, you must send to me, and the other two copies you must put with the papers I sent to you today. Then send everything to this address:
>
> HQ Northern Area Command
>
> AP0757
>
> US Army
>
> Frankfurt am Main
>
> Unfortunately, I do not have any more time to write. I will write you a long letter on Sunday, my dear little Anita. Heartfelt greetings and many tender kisses from your Heinz.

Fortunately, after another five months, I had gotten permission from the West German and the United States governments to leave. When I finally got a letter in the mail stating that I had permission and all the paperwork, I had been in West Germany for exactly one year. It was December 1956, and I purchased my ticket from a travel agency to take an ocean liner, the SS America, from Bremerhoffen, Germany, to New York. Bremerhoffen is a seaport in the northern part of Germany.

"There is one spot left on the boat that leaves December 10th, but you would be in the lower deck, is that OK?" asked the travel agent. I nodded in acknowledgement. "And your roommate is black: are you OK with that?" she asked me.

"Yes, that is fine with me," I said. Although most Germans did not know any black people personally, I had become very good friends with the two black men in my father's band in Frohburg. The men were kind and fun, and we often entertained them in our home—my father would bring them home after they played in a club or at an affair, and my Mama would feed them and offer whatever she had. My Papa never told her ahead of time, but my Mama had come to expect this. They always told my Mama what a wonderful cook she was, even if she served them only potato soup. Papa never thought about the fact that we barely had anything to eat ourselves; he just wanted to be nice to them. So I had no problem with a black roommate on the boat. I bought the ticket and went back to Elizabeth Krankenhaus, the hospital.

The next morning, which was December 1st, I told the Oberschwester that I had a ticket for the boat on December 10th. On December 7th, after I had finished my last laundry shift, Oberschwester Hildegard invited me down to her office. She asked me to sit down across from her desk.

"I have a little something for you, Anita," she said, as she handed me a wrapped gift. I felt my face flush, I was so embarrassed. I opened the box, but I still felt so uncomfortable, like I didn't deserve the gift. As I opened the box, I saw a pink cookbook with a picture of a slim blonde German hausfrau, wearing an apron and preparing dinner over a stove. The gift was so kind, I thought. She knew I was going to get married. Inside the cover, the head nun had written, "Anita, wish you a wonderful life and much happiness in America." I kept this book through all the years as a reminder of this wonderful group of women who meant so much to me and gave me so much hope when I came to West Germany.

The next day, I packed my worldly possessions in the bag that Frau Schiller had given me almost one year ago. I had the same two outfits I had taken out of East Germany plus one new one that I had purchased, my coat, two pairs of shoes, one nightgown, one slip, underwear, the book from Oberschwester Hildegard, and the New Testament Bible that Helmut's mother had given me. I was elated that everything still fit in that same bag. I had a small purse that I had purchased in Oberhausen for my passport and visa. I wrote to Heinz and to my Mama.

As I walked out of the hospital towards the train station, I was excited this time. The fear I experienced when I left East Germany a year ago was not there; now my feelings were that of excitement and anticipation of a new adventure and of going to America. I tried to imagine what America was like, but I could not. Heinz told me it is so huge, but I could not imagine it. I thought of my family again: I wondered if my family would ever be allowed to leave East Germany and visit other countries.

*****

"Yet the LORD longs to be gracious to you; he rises to show you compassion. For the LORD is a God of justice. Blessed are all who wait for him!" Isaiah 30:18

Heinz, as a child, probably only three or four years old, with his father, Paul. Even though Heinz was raised for the first six years of his life by his grandparents, Paul made every effort to see his son as often as possible, until he married and was able to raise him with his new wife, Marta.

Heinz's family: Onkel Wilhelm, Tante Berta (Heinz's Aunt), Heinz, his father, Paul, with Paul's father, August, seated. This picture was taken when Wilhelm visited Germany after the war.

Renate and me: Renate is about three years old and I am six.

The day I was confirmed at age 14, on Palm Sunday in 1946 in the Saint Michaelis Lutheran Church in Frohburg, Germany.

Erika, Papa, Renate, Mama, and Karl-Heinz; only my older brother Hans is missing because he was at college: this is the last picture I have of my whole family together before I fled East Germany.

This is me at work in a factory that made building materials. I worked in their quality control lab in East Germany before I escaped to West Berlin and then to Frankfurt on my way to America.

Me and Heinz: This was our engagement picture taken in a studio in West Germany in 1956, the summer he visited me in West Germany.

PART II

A NEW LIFE —IN A NEW COUNTRY

—5—

Sailing to the United States

I was overwhelmed by the size of the SS America. The boat carried about 500 people. As I walked up to the ocean liner, I could hardly see it from one end to the other. As I stepped onto the boat with my small bag of belongings, I saw myself leaving the valleys of Nazism, Communism, and poverty behind me. On the path ahead, I saw a perfect life with Heinz and hopefully many children to follow. I was optimistic and excited.

Here is the first and only letter I wrote to Heinz from the boat, on United States Lines Stationery:

> 11.12.56
>
> My dear good Heinz,
>
> Now my dearest one, I am going to write you the first lines from the boat I am on. I can barely believe that we will see each other in nine days from now. It is for me, a feeling I cannot even describe. However, my Heinz, I want to tell you everything in

chronological order. First of all, I would like to thank you for your dear letter, which you sent to my friend Dorla.[3] Heinz, I waited for the suitcase from your aunt until Saturday and then I had to go to Hamburg. I could not wait any longer. I wrote to your aunt one more time from Hamburg and I hope that she understood. She wrote to me that a Christmas present for her Philadelphia relatives would be in the suitcase. However, I could not miss the boat because the suitcase did not arrive in time. But I do not want to be upset about the suitcase any longer. It already upset me enough. I will talk to you about everything when we get together.

I spent Saturday with Dorla in Hamburg. On Sunday morning, we went to church and somehow I felt peace after the service that everything would be OK. Monday morning, I checked my luggage at the harbor, and then I had to spend some time with the all the paperwork. My nerves were shot, besides being nervous; you know how much I hate paperwork. I was a bundle of nerves. I was so upset, I am sure you never saw anything like it. In the evening at 17:38, we went with a special train, which took us from Hamburg to the ship in Bremerhoffen. I said good-bye to Dorla in Hamburg. I'm so glad she was there to help me and keep my company through these last few days until it was time to go. Heinz, can you imagine if my Mama would have been with me until all the way to Bremerhoffen? I believe she would not have been able to handle seeing me get on this boat. In a way, I was truly glad that

I was by myself. At least I did not have to wave to anybody from the boat.

At 12:05, the ship left Germany. I shared a cabin with a black person. The cabin was very small; however, the ship was like a luxury boat to me. You know what, Heinz, as a prevention, I took some seasick pills along; however, nothing helped, and I got so seasick. This morning, I was so sick and I had to, whether I wanted to or not, empty the contents of my stomach. I tried so hard to control myself, but it does not help a lot. At that moment, I feel a little bit better, and I ate a little bit for *Mittagessens* (lunch), but I will be very happy when I will see you again, and I will be very glad to have the sea experience behind me. A thousand times more would I have liked it, if we could have gone together, my good dear Heinz. (*Mein Guter*).

I already wrote to your Tante Else before I left Oberhausen. Heinz, I beg you, be a dear and get from the United States lines, a paper that you pick me up directly from the boat. I understand that this piece of paper gives you the opportunity to go to the gate. *Mein Guter*, that Tante Marie wants to come with you to pick me up, that is nice, so I will get to know her earlier, before I meet everyone else.

Heinz, my handwriting is atrocious today, but please don't be upset, I hope you can decipher it somehow. My pen's ink is dripping out, and I do not write well with this type of pen. And I still feel so lightheaded.

My cabin roommate is very nice. She speaks a little German, and we can understand each other a little bit. Oh Heinz, even though the separation from Germany was not an easy thing to do, I am looking forward to our life together. Heinz, please do not forget to send my parents a silver wedding anniversary card. I think about you all the time and dream of our future together. I am so happy that we can celebrate Christmas together. Oh Heinz, my heart is overflowing with excitement, and I could write so much more, but I want to tell you in person. In one week, a thousand sweet kisses and heartfelt greetings from your little Anita. Please also greet your relatives from me.

Almost everyone on the boat was leaving West Germany permanently to start a new life in America. The trip was supposed to take nine days; actually, it took ten days because they had to stop the boat to do an emergency appendectomy on a middle-aged man. After the first day, I began to get seasick. I couldn't walk onto the deck without throwing up. I stayed in my cabin most of the time, which was depressing. My roommate, Michelle, was an African-American from New York. She was a beautiful young woman in her twenties, very tall and thin. She was a singer and had just traveled through all of West Germany and was returning to America. I could hardly speak to her, but she had a German-English dictionary, and sign language helped.

Sunrises in the early morning cheered me up, but I couldn't enjoy them for long without running back to my cabin. Because I was traveling with the cheapest rates, I did not have the privilege of using a chair on the deck. One afternoon, an elderly Austrian gentleman with gray hair and a walrus-like mustache saw me vomiting into a bag. I was on an indoor deck, and I must have looked terrible.

"How are you, *Fraulein*?" he asked, after I had settled down a bit. We were standing on the deck. I was holding onto the rail.

"You look all white, can I do anything for you?" he asked.

I talked to him for a while and told him all that had happened to me in the last year, and the man was impressed. He offered to buy me dinner in one of the nicer restaurants that evening. I refused, feeling as though I didn't deserve it and I would never be able to pay him back. Later that evening, I heard a knock on my cabin door. I opened the door to an attendant from the boat crew. She informed me that this man had purchased a chair for me to use on the upper deck. At least then I could get some fresh air. I was so touched, I just started to cry. Why would a perfect stranger be so kind to me? I never had the chance to thank him.

Throughout the ten days, I got to know some of the people on the boat. One girl was leaving Germany to get married to her boyfriend who was already in California. She had also escaped from East Germany: she was originally from Leipzig. She was a very pretty blonde girl, about five years younger than me. She fled by taking the subway in Berlin—-because people took the subway back and forth between East and West Berlin all the time, it was pretty easy to do, she said. No one was really checking or asking too many questions once you got on the U-Bahn.

I also met another young girl named Inge, about twenty years old, who had lost both parents during the war. She was going to Arizona to work as an au pair for an American family. She had no family in Germany, so she thought it was best to make a new life for herself somewhere else. She was originally from the Bodensee area of Germany, in the southern part near Switzerland. I also met three nuns who were originally from West Germany. They had moved to America before the beginning of WWII and had come back to Germany for a visit. They were very nice; all three of them were really overweight. I talked to them for a while and told them of my plans. "Look here," they told me, "eat some of this rye bread now, you won't find good bread like this in the America." I laughed but didn't bother to eat any of it since I didn't keep much food down anyway. At the end of the ten days on the boat, I lost about 10 pounds.

I thought of Heinz often. My Mama always felt sorry for him because he never had a real childhood. I was so confident that as we navigated the path of life together as a team, he would be completely happy. I really believed that we were meant to be together.

*****

As the boat got closer to NYC, I became very anxious. I could hear the traffic noise and clamor from the city. The blaring sounds, the clatter, horns honking, and massive car engine noises were all unfamiliar to me. As the boat pulled into New York's harbor, my heart began to beat so fast I could hear it in my ears. I am not sure if my head was spinning from the nausea or from my teeming emotions. From the upper deck, I could see the skyscrapers, also a new sight for my eyes. I had never seen buildings so high before.

Once the boat stopped, we were all instructed to go back to our cabin to gather our belongings. The announcements were being made in both English and German. My stomach was in knots. I tried to say good-bye to Michelle and wanted to wish her good luck with her singing, but I wasn't sure of the words. Michelle motioned with her hands for me to keep her dictionary. Michelle and I then hugged each other, nothing was spoken, but the message of wishing each other the best was communicated nonetheless. I put the dictionary in my bag, too.

I was one of the last people off the boat, as women with children went first, then U. S. citizens, then those with first-class tickets, and last were those of us on the lower deck. I felt awkward as I walked off the boat, not quite sure of my footing. I was probably still seasick. My legs felt like wooden poles, which I willed to move one stick at a time. I just had trouble walking as my body adjusted to the fact that the boat had stopped moving. The salty tears in my eyes made each step through the crowds even more difficult.

Finally, as I walked down the ramp the boat, I anxiously scanned the crowds for Heinz. The fresh cool December air helped pushed me along, too. I then remembered that it was my Mama's birthday, and I started to cry even harder. It was December 20, 1956. I kept looking so intensely through the crowd of people, my eyes began to hurt. Where could Heinz be, I thought? I looked at all the men again to see if I might have missed him, when an elderly lady, with clear glasses and wrinkles that looked like deep pen marks, called to me in German.

"Is that you, Anita?" she called, in a very husky German voice. She introduced herself as Heinz's aunt, Tante Else. She was only a little taller than me, and she had very curly short hair. She reminded me of one of my Mama's sisters. She immediately explained that Heinz was unable to meet the boat. Heinz had taken the previous day off from work, but since the boat was a day late, he could not get off from his job again. It made sense, but I was so disheartened that Heinz was not there.

Tante Else was married to Fritz, Heinz's uncle who sponsored me to come to the United States. "How did you recognize me?" I asked.

"Well, Heinz had a few pictures that he showed me. And I figured you would be one of the last ones off the boat," she said. I was still so disappointed that Heinz was not there, and I was slow to comprehend what Tante Else was instructing me to do. "So, Anita, we need to get on the train to go back to Philadelphia, but first we need to get a cab back to the train station." Tante Else waved money in her hand as she hailed a cab. I thought it was so strange to see someone waving money around like that.

Once we got in to the cab, I was completely amazed by what my eyes were taking in. I had never seen so many cars, so many people, and so much activity. My ears were not accustomed to the volume. I smelled the hot dogs from the corner vendors, a smell that was unfamiliar.

Tante Else started up a conversation with me in the cab. "Your future husband already has an apartment, but you can stay with Fritz and me until you two are married. You need to go to the Lutheran church and get married there. It is in the Feltonville section of Philadelphia, and the pastor there speaks German, so you can get married without having to learn English. And you will need to buy a wedding dress," she said quickly. I had no idea what she was talking about. What was the Feltonville section of Philadelphia? At least Heinz and I could get married in German. I was glad about that. Heinz had never mentioned a Lutheran church with a German pastor in any of his letters. I didn't even know how to answer her. She continued to talk about everything that needed to be done, but I was at least three steps behind her. I was so tired.

Once we got out of the cab, Tante Else paid the driver and then we walked into the train station to get a train back to Philadelphia. At the train station, the people, newsstands, vendors, magazine shops, bakeries, and coffee shops were sights that I had never seen—at least not this many people in the same small space. I still felt like I had to vomit: my stomach had not yet settled from the boat. "Ok," said Tante Else, "you sit here while I find out what track our train is on." Tante Else then bought me a bagel and a soda. I had never had a bagel or soda before. I liked the bagel, but the soda made my stomach feel even worse, so I did not finish it.

"Ok, Anita," Tante Else said a few minutes later. "Our train will leave in one hour, so we have to just sit here." To me, it seemed like Tante Else was moving at lightning speed, while I was just trying to understand how so many people could be in the train station at the same time. I tried to read some of the English signs and could decode only a few words, like coffee, based on the picture and because it was close to the German word, *Kaffee*.

Fritz and Wilhelm lived near each other and were quite close. Both were Heinz's father's brothers, and both had come to the United States after WWI. Fritz had married Tante Else in Germany, and they both came to the America together. Wilhelm had married an American woman named Marie.

I then asked Tante Else how Heinz was doing. "Oh, do not worry, Anita. Heinz will be at our house for dinner tonight," said Tante Else. "I am going to make a nice German dinner for all of us." Tante Else was talking so fast, I still could barely keep up.

Once we got on the train to Philadelphia, Tante Else slowed down a little bit. Tante Else was probably just nervous, too. After all, she had never met me before, and she wanted to have things go smoothly. Then Tante Else began to tell me of her experiences and how hard it was to adjust to the American culture and the difficulty of learning the language. She told me she had two daughters, one who was already married.

At 30th Street Station, the main train station in downtown Philadelphia, I was amazed at all the stores and places to eat. I had never seen Chinese people before. Nor had I ever seen so many black people. It was overwhelming. It helped me to understand how large and diverse America was and is. It was also very cold as we walked outside to get the bus and then a trolley to Tante Else's house, which was located on Rising Sun Avenue and Levick Street in Philadelphia—not the downtown part of Philadelphia, but still in the city. "This is the last thing we have to take, Anita, and then you'll be at my house," said Tante Else.

*****

"Your path led through the sea, your way through the mighty waters, though your footprints were not seen." Psalm 77:19

—6—

Reuniting with Heinz—and Getting Married!

Tante Else graciously invited me into her row home in the northeast section of Philadelphia. I was really surprised to see homes with flat roofs in Philadelphia. The homes in Germany did not have flat roofs. Tante Else's house was nice: there were arched room dividers and white walls with a lot of pictures of Tante Else with her children. Tante Else had a nice living room, with a blue love seat and a coffee table and a bay window, with Hummel figures on the ledge. She invited me to sit down while she tended to dinner in the kitchen. She had a television, which I had never seen before; I had seen movies in Germany, but the television was just fascinating to me. I could not believe that you could actually see someone delivering the news like that. I was mesmerized when the news anchor started to talk about the weather, and they showed all kinds of maps. I had no idea what they were saying, but it was fun to watch.

After a few minutes, Tante Else came out of the kitchen and took me to the back room where I was to stay for the next few days. Tante Else and Onkel Fritz owned a dry-goods store which occupied the bottom part of their home. It was right before Christmas, and I was amazed at how Americans put lights all over their lawn, windows, and houses. I had never seen anything like that before. In Germany, sometimes real candles were put on the tree, but never lights in the windows. I thought it was so beautiful.

A few minutes later, I heard a knock on the door. My heart jumped, and I could feel the blood rush to my face. I couldn't wait to see Heinz again. I rushed to the door and opened it. There he stood, just as handsome as ever. He was smiling. As Heinz entered, I began to sob, I could not help it. I was so happy to see him and so drained from the boat and the long trip from New York to Philadelphia. "I thought you would be happy to see me, Anita, not cry?" said Heinz seriously, not jokingly. Heinz did not understand my overwhelming emotions. He kissed me. For me, I felt like I had someone in this world again. "Now that's enough of that, you two," yelled Tante Else from the kitchen. "Dinner is ready." She invited us to sit down around her table in the kitchen. She had a beautiful red table cloth for Christmas with a thick white candle in a gold base for the centerpiece.

Fritz had come in by this time, too. He warmly welcomed me to America and shook my hand. We all sat down to eat sauerkraut with pork, German potato salad, and rolls. Germans really like to eat starchy vegetables like potatoes, and Tante Else's 30 years in America hadn't changed her much. Later, I learned that most of the Germans who had settled in the Philadelphia tried to hold onto their culture.

During dinner, Heinz talked about the apartment, his job as a cabinet maker/carpenter, and how we should get married as soon as possible. As Heinz started to talk about the wedding, Tante Else interrupted him and told us how we should go about it. I knew she was just trying to help: after all, she had been in Philadelphia for a long time, and she knew that Heinz's English was not the best. Onkel Fritz seemed to be a very kind man, but very quiet. He said almost nothing the entire meal. Occasionally, he had Tante Else bring him another beer, and she picked up the napkin that dropped off his lap. That was our German culture. The women served the men and didn't complain about it. I was so glad that Heinz wasn't really like that. He has never demanded anything from me; he has only been kind and caring.

"You need to go to Pastor Bauer at Feltonville Church tomorrow," said Tante Else to Heinz.

"I cannot take another day off from work right now, Tante Else," said Heinz.

"Ok, then Heinz, I will call Pastor Bauer at Feltonville Lutheran Church tomorrow, and I will arrange a meeting for the two of you," said Else, as she began to clear the dishes from the table. I was glad Tante Else knew what to do and I was glad that she was helping us, but she did seem to be bossing us around. I didn't really like that, but I didn't say anything because I was so happy to be with Heinz. And his aunts, uncles, and cousins in Philadelphia were the only family we had in America. I was determined to get along with everyone. In a few short weeks, we will be married, I thought.

My attention turned back to the food that tasted so good. I was surprised to see the huge portions of food that Tante Else, Onkel Fritz, and Heinz ate. What we had for dinner between the four of us that evening would have lasted my family for an entire week.

That night, I tossed and turned in my bed. Here I was in America, a free country, and finally reunited with Heinz after six years. I couldn't believe it! I looked out the window from my bedroom. It was a clear night and an almost full moon. The moon glowed and smiled back at me. I longed to be able to speak to my Mama, to tell her that I was in America and that I was safe. My heart ached for her, and I hoped that everything was OK at home. Karli was six this year for Christmas, and I wondered if he would even think about me this year.

*****

The next morning, I looked out my bedroom window, and I saw a white Volkswagen hit another car. Following that, a lot of yelling in English, and then police cars came. Police was also close to the German word *Polizei*, so I learned that word right away. This accident really upset me. It should not have, it had nothing to do with me personally, but somehow, my perfect ideal about life in America was stained. It was naïve of me, I realize that now, but I just did not want to experience anything that could be the least bit distressing, at least not right away.

While Heinz was at work, Tante Else and Tante Marie took me over to a large department store to pick out my wedding dress. I had never seen a store like that before. The noise, the number of people all crowded into the store, and the smells, like the perfume counter, awakened my senses. I liked watching the Americans look at the clothes. All the Americans were very friendly to me. When I tried to tell the saleslady that I wanted to try on a dress, she was very patient. I found this to be true all the time. I tried on a few dresses, but none were to my liking. I had always been chubby, and since I was short, too, it was not so easy to find something that would fit. Although I enjoyed the attention that Tante Else and Tante Marie were lavishing on me, I thought of my Mama and Renate and how they should be here with me. It was painful not to share the happy moments with them. Tante Else and Tante Marie were being as nice as possible, yet they were not really family, at least not to me, yet.

My emotional pendulum swung from happiness over the fact that I was getting married to sadness over having left a very loving family behind. As kind as Tante Else was, she was not at all like my Mama. I really didn't want Tante Else to plan my wedding, but I just felt like she was being so nice to me, I just wanted to agree with all of her suggestions. So I tried to make the best of it, and I continued to try on dresses.

The next day, we went to John Wanamaker's in another part of Philadelphia. The dresses there were a bit more expensive. Tante Marie really wanted to pay for the wedding dress. She really did not speak much German, so Tante Else translated for me. I followed Tante Else and Tante Marie into the department stores, where the signs and directions made no sense. After going to those stores, I knew that English school needed to be on the top of my list. Tante Else and Tante Marie did all the talking in English when we went into the dressing rooms.

At Wanamaker's, I found a plain copper-colored dress; it wasn't a wedding dress, but I didn't know I was supposed to be picking out a long white gown. I thought we would just have a civil ceremony anyway. Tante Else and Tante Marie had directed me to dresses that they thought might look nice on me. We were probably in a plus-size section of the department store. I just could not read any of the signs. That's where I found the copper-colored dress. I tried it on, and it fit me well. It was bought and packed up. Tante Marie paid for it, and I thanked her in German. Heinz's aunts really wanted to make me comfortable, and for that, I was so grateful.

Next, Tante Else decided to buy me some shoes, and she paid for them also. Their kindness was so overwhelming. Tante Else also picked out a hat to go with the dress: it had feathers and sequins on it, and it matched the color of my dress. She suggested that Heinz could pay for that. We bought it, and I assume that she asked Heinz to pay her back.

When Heinz got home that night, he came to Tante Else's to have dinner with us. "Heinz, do you want to see the dress we bought today for the wedding?" I asked him.

"*Ach, nein*, Anita. I can wait. But Tante Else, thank you for taking Anita to the stores," said Heinz. "I will have to call Tante Marie tonight and thank her, too," he added. Heinz never had any patience for looking at dresses, even my wedding dress. Those details that are important to women just seemed trivial to him.

Later that week, Heinz and I drove over to meet Pastor Bauer at Feltonville Lutheran Church. The church was also in the Feltonville section of Philadelphia, right off Roosevelt Boulevard, a main highway in the city of Philadelphia. The dark gray church building was very large—it took up one whole block—and it had a tall steeple and bells that rang on Sunday mornings. The church had an English and then a German service every Sunday morning. Since so many German immigrants settled in the Feltonville section of Philadelphia the German service was more crowded than the English service.

The church had a house right on the premises for the pastor, so he lived there, too. He invited us into to sit down at his kitchen table, and he offered us a cup of coffee. It was still in the early evening. Pastor Bauer was in his late 40s and was almost completely bald and gray. He was a big man, tall and heavy. His voice was deep and commanding. He was originally from somewhere in West Germany;

I cannot remember the name of the town. Heinz had never met him before.

"So, your aunt tells me you want to get married. That is so nice. How long have you been in the Feltonville section of Philadelphia, Heinz?" he asked.

"Oh, about a year and a half," said Heinz.

Then he asked me some questions. "Anita, where did you go to church in Germany?"

"Well, I went to Saint Michaelis Kirche in Frohburg after the war, but as I got older, we went only on Easter and Christmas. Eventually, my family stopped going altogether. For me, it was when I was 15; I was then too old for the choir. After Communism took over in East Germany, church was not encouraged. Hardly anyone was going to church there anymore," I explained.

"That is such a shame," replied Pastor Bauer. His scrunched his face; I could not tell if he disapproved of my honesty or not.

"So, Heinz, do you have a job?" he asked, looking directly at Heinz.

Heinz started moving around in his seat a little bit and starting tapping his fingers on the table. "I have a temporary job right now. I know I will get this permanent union job in just a few days," he answered, but his voice was uneven. I knew he was uncomfortable.

"What, you do not have a permanent job? Well, I cannot marry the two of you until you have a permanent job, Heinz," he said. I was very upset at this point. I did not want any more delays. But I said nothing. Pastor Bauer continued, "Now listen, I have a friend who can hire you. Here is his name and number. Give him a call tomorrow." Pastor Bauer's voice got louder and louder, and his face started to get red.

Heinz's face was red, too. He did not even answer him. And I could not believe this was happening.

"Ok, then, let me know when you are set up, and then we'll make arrangements for a wedding," said Pastor Bauer triumphantly.

We shook hands, said good night, and we promised to call him back in a few days. On the way home, Heinz was so upset. He knew that the union job was only a few days away, and he did not want to call someone to ask for a favor. I did not really know what to say. I never expected Pastor Bauer to delay the wedding like that. I thought I would be free in America, but very soon, I realized that when you depend on other people so much, you really could not be free. Separately, Heinz and I both resolved to become independent and stand on our own feet as quickly as possible.

On Saturday, Heinz wanted to buy me a present for Christmas, so we took the train into downtown Philadelphia and went to John Wanamaker's department store, but this was the main store in the downtown part of Philadelphia (the other store we had gone to was in the Northeast section). This was my first trip into center city Philadelphia. The tall buildings in the city of Philadelphia also overwhelmed me. I stood there and looked up at them: to me, they did not seem real. This was now my third time to a department store, and it still seemed like I was dreaming. "Why don't you pick out a skirt for yourself, Anita? I'll walk around the store for a bit, and then I'll come and find you," said Heinz.

When Heinz found me, I was in the maternity section looking at some skirts.

"Anita, you need to get out of here, this is the maternity section," he said with a nervous look on his face. His face got bright tomato red. He was so embarrassed. I thought it was so funny. I could not read the signs. But Heinz did not laugh. Then Heinz took me over to the right section and stayed with me until I found a skirt.

*****

Tante Else kept the German traditions by going to church on Christmas Eve and then having a meal. Germans open up their gifts on Christmas Eve, and Tante Else and her family still did that. Heinz had given me some money so I could buy gifts for Tante Else and Onkel Fritz and also for Onkel Wilhelm and Tante Marie. The day before, Tante Else took me to the local stores in northeast Philadelphia and picked out a bottle of perfume. Onkel Fritz, she said, could use some new socks. She also picked out some after-shave for Onkel Wilhelm and a wallet for Tante Marie. I had no idea how far the money Heinz gave me would go, but Tante Else knew, and she kindly directed me to items that we could be afford. I enjoyed being in the malls, and I liked trying to talk to the Americans. Everyone was so patient and accepting.

We had a nice dinner with Onkel Fritz and Tante Else for Christmas. Their daughters and son-in-law came over, too. Everyone was very welcoming and kind to me. They brought gifts for Heinz and me. It was so sweet. Tante Else sensed how much I missed my own family, and she did her best to help us establish new traditions. Onkel Fritz and Tante Else had unconsciously become surrogate parents to Heinz and me.

I enjoyed learning about the American Christmas traditions. The stores were filled with Christmas trees with lights, wreaths, and garlands. I saw children waiting in line to see Santa Claus. Tante Else explained that Americans celebrate on Christmas morning, which was one American custom she could never get used to. For Germans, the entire season of Christmas is celebrated, beginning with the four advents, which are the four Sundays leading up to Christmas. It is a special time for families, who sing songs on each advent and light candles for each advent: one candle for the first Sunday in December, two for the next, and so on.

Germans also celebrate Saint Nicholas Day, which falls on December 6th. Little kids put their shoes by the door the night before, hoping that Saint Nicholas, one of Santa's helpers, will fill their shoes with treats of chocolates and other goodies. German Christmas celebrations and traditions were not so religious based, but from what I could tell, neither were the American traditions.

A few days after Christmas, people just started coming over to Tante Else's house. First Tante Marie, Wilhelm's wife, then Tante Else's daughters, then a few of Tante Else's neighbors. I had not met any of her neighbors yet. Tante Else explained in German that I was having a shower for my wedding, and that it was an American tradition. All the ladies had gifts for me, and Tante Else made a lot of food. Tante Else also served Italian sausage: I had never tasted that before. I thought it was delicious. I was so embarrassed, but I so appreciated all that Tante Else had done for me.

After everyone ate, Tante Else directed me to a chair in her living room and asked me to start opening all the gifts. Some of her neighbors had given me sexy lingerie—my cheeks turned bright red—this definitely wasn't something the Germans would do, I thought. Others gave me pots and pans, towels, bed sheets, and small kitchen gadgets. I asked Tante Else to thank them all for me. I was beginning to learn more words: thank you, you are welcome, hi, bye, good night. These gestures of kindness just overwhelmed me. Since I had no family, everything that Tante Else did just meant so much to me.

When Heinz got home from work, I tried to show him everything. He didn't have the patience to look at all the gifts, but he did make a point of thanking Tante Else for having the shower.

The following day, on Saturday, Heinz and I went to city hall to have a civil ceremony and get married. I wore the copper-colored dress. I did not really know how well Heinz spoke English because we were always speaking German with each other. "We want to get married," Heinz must have said to the clerk in City Hall. The next thing I knew, we both put our hands on the Bible and signed some documents. We both thought we had gotten married. Heinz and I went back to Tante Else's house to show her the documents and tell her what happened.

"You two are so stupid," she said in German. "You are not married; all you did is apply for a marriage license. You still have to go to Pastor Bauer, like I told you, to get married," she continued. Heinz felt so stupid, but I just laughed. "Well, Anita, you might as well get used to the American culture and way of doing things," said Tante Else, in between her own controlled bouts of laughter.

A few days later, on my wedding day, I walked down the aisle at Feltonville Lutheran Church, alone. I was wearing the copper-colored dress with the hat and a pair of heavy pantyhose that I had borrowed from Tante Else. It was January 19, 1957, and I had been in America for a month. Germans have both the bride and groom walk down the aisle together, so the American tradition was strange to me, that of the father walking his daughter down the aisle. Tante Else's daughter Rosemary was my only bridesmaid. Billy, Onkel Wilhelm's son and Heinz's first cousin, was Heinz's best man.

Tante Else took some pictures. Heinz's few cousins, his uncles, and Tante Else's neighbors were there, about 20 people in all. The church was old with stained-glass windows, but the inside was dark. The pulpit was several steps above the pews, and behind Pastor Bauer, there was a large Crucifix of Jesus, made of dark wood.

Pastor Bauer wore a black robe with a purple sash across the top and had a large chain with a thick gold cross hanging from his neck. I hoped God would bless our life together.

As I stood by myself at the back of the church, I was sad that only 20 people were there to witness our marriage. As the organ music started to play, my tears just surrendered. I saw Heinz standing at the altar, all alone. He looked so handsome and confident. Tears trickled down my face for the rest of the day. I missed my family so much; I actually felt pains in my chest. I just wished my Mama could have been there to see me. And my sisters, too.

We got through the vows and the short, twenty-minute ceremony. Pastor Bauer had asked us what our confirmation verses were. Heinz could not remember his confirmation verse. But I remembered mine: it was 1 John 2:17, *"The world and its desires pass away, but man who does the will of God lives forever."* Pastor Bauer developed a short message around this verse. I honestly do not remember what he said; I only know that he used my confirmation verse.

Then I saw how proud Heinz was when Pastor Bauer announced that we were man and wife. We turned to face our twenty guests, and they all stood up and applauded.

As we exited the door, I was surprised when people starting throwing rice at us. That was a strange American custom. I had no idea what was happening. In Germany, children hold a ribbon on both sides of the door, blocking the bride and groom from exiting, until someone gives them a scissors to cut the ribbon. Then the groom throws coins to the little kids, which is supposed to bring luck.

Afterwards, everyone was invited back to Tante Else's house for a turkey dinner that Tante Marie had made. I had never tasted turkey before, but I thought it was delicious. It never felt like a party to me because I knew hardly anyone there, but I was so grateful to Tante Else and Tante Marie for trying to make it a special day for me.

I then moved into Heinz's apartment, but we had no honeymoon. Heinz had just started a new job with the union and he could not take any time off. When I saw the apartment, I felt so guilty for my family in East Germany. Heinz rented an apartment on Eleanor Street in Philadelphia from Mr. and Mrs. Smith, who owned the building and lived downstairs. Our apartment had three rooms: one bedroom, a living room, a bathroom with a tub, and an eat-in kitchen. The Smiths had provided a small refrigerator. The apartment was very clean. The walls were painted white. Heinz had a bedroom set already; it was all light-gray furniture with a dresser and a mirror. Heinz also had a small brown sofa and a small television on a small cart. His kitchen table had been an old table that Tante Else no longer needed. The table was square and had a white Formica top with two white wooden chairs that Heinz had recently re-painted. We had dishes and utensils from the shower and from what Heinz had bought previously. We had more than enough.

Mr. and Mrs. Smith were very excited to meet me. We could not communicate, but their friendly demeanor was inviting. Mr. and

Mrs. Smith were in their late 50s, their children were grown. Mr. Smith was thin and bald, with a kind face and smile. Mrs. Smith wore glasses and always kept her brown and graying hair up in a bun. When I had a question, I had no problem knocking on Mrs. Smith's door to ask it. She enjoyed helping me. She often took me to the local stores in Feltonville and tried to teach me the English words along the way. We used sign language, and when that failed, I tried to draw on a piece of paper. It never mattered to her how long it took, she was very patient with me. I followed her around all the time.

Right after our wedding, I wrote to my Mama. I told her in that letter that I was so happy that I had come to America, that I was fine, and that I did not regret my decision to leave East Germany. When my Mama wrote back a few weeks later, she told me that my last sentence was crossed out, but she could tell what I was trying to say. After that, I was careful about what I wrote in letters to my Mama. A few times I tried to send money. Fortunately, the money that I sent always got there.

After a few days of marriage, Heinz realized that he needed to pay $50 in union dues. That was all the money we had in the bank. Heinz asked me if he should ask one of his uncles for the money.

"Oh Heinz, I just don't know. If we use the $50, we won't even have any money for groceries until you get paid again. Maybe we should ask them for a loan," I said. I knew Tante Else would not have minded at all. Heinz ultimately decided to use his own money and never asked either of his uncles. We drank water and ate soup for one week. I would have asked for the loan, but I did not want to start a fight with Heinz over it.

*****

"Therefore, do not worry about tomorrow, for tomorrow will worry about itself. Each day has enough trouble of its own."
Matthew 6: 34

—7—

Starting Our New Lives Together

Once Heinz got paid again, he took me food shopping at the local grocery store. I had never been in such a large food store. I was overwhelmed by how much there was to buy. I had never even seen or used a shopping cart before. The abundance that surrounded me was almost embarrassing. Even on Heinz's relatively small income, we were able to enjoy so much variety of food and in quantities that would have fed my whole family of seven in Germany. Because my family never had a refrigerator, we went shopping for milk and groceries every day. Meats were cooked the same day they were bought. Sometimes, we could keep things cold in the basement. Potatoes were stored there for the winter. My Mama boiled milk each day and let it cool; we drank it later. So, buying this quantity of food was an overwhelming experience for me.

As I turned the corner with the cart, I knocked down a pie. Heinz was embarrassed and quickly picked it up, while I just joked about how I needed to learn to steer better. There were so many vegetables and fruits. Broccoli and squash seemed strange. I never bought them, I had no idea how I would have cooked them. When we went to the meat section, I was overwhelmed by how much frozen meat was available. Steak and ribs were meats that we never had. We bought a week's worth of food, and I had never done that before.

I knew I needed to find work, but I couldn't really speak any English. Fortunately, Olney High School was within walking distance from our apartment, and I signed up for evening English classes there. When I arrived, my class was full: there were 30 students. Some were from Cuba, Japan, Poland, and Russia. There was no one else from Germany. No one could speak English, and the class was conducted in English. It was a terrible way to learn: mostly, the teachers used pictures and words together to teach the students. I felt lonely there since I really couldn't communicate with anyone. I needed a friend, and I needed to feel like I belonged.

One night in English class, I was asked to read out loud. Since most everyone I had interacted with was Heinz and his aunts and uncles, and they were all still speaking to me in German, I really did not know how to pronounce anything. My face turned bright red. Ok, I thought to myself, I'll try. "The girl usually wears red," I pronounced it as "*se girrrll ew su alley wheres ret*." The class roared. How did all those other foreigners know that I was wrong? I just sat there and waited for the instructor to repeat the sentence.

*****

The next time I went shopping, I was alone and so I struggled. It was only one block from our apartment, so I could walk there. I never saw white bread before, and to me, it tasted like spider webs. Most of the vegetables were those I had never seen, either: eggplant, broccoli, squash, and zucchini. Corn on the cob was horse food, to me. I stuck to potatoes, pasta, and meats for Heinz. But it was fun to watch other people shop. I started to memorize the names of foods: bread was close to *brot*; milk was close to *milch*, so those were easy for me to learn. And putting names and pictures together really helped.

One day, Heinz complained while we were eating dinner because the rolls had some kind of cheese in them. This had not been on the picture, and so I had no idea.

"What is this cheese in these rolls, Anita? That tastes terrible," he said. I felt so small when he criticized me like that. I was able to maintain my sense of humor through these blunders because I was learning a new culture and I would eventually find my way in this land; however, Heinz seemed to have lost any sense of humor or adventure about our experience. When he criticized, he was harsh and angry. It frightened me, and I didn't want to cause that reaction. I felt really insecure because I could never be sure what would trigger him, so I just did my best to keep him calm and peaceful.

"I will never buy them again, Heinz, I am so sorry. What kind would you like me to buy the next time?"

I also made Heinz his lunches, three small sandwiches with liverwurst and mustard on rye bread, and a few cookies. Heinz liked to eat frequent small meals; if he didn't, he would get a headache. Heinz also wanted to eat as soon as he got home from work. He would often get angry if dinner was not on the table as soon as he got in: "Where is the meal, Anita? You know how hungry I am when I get home. "Why isn't the soup hot enough? You are going to have to reheat it right when you hear that I am coming in," he would almost be yelling when he said those things. I was taken aback by his demeanor, but I never said anything about it. I just tried to overlook it because for Germans, the husband is in charge and the wife should never complain.

But sometimes, it was really hard being a good German housewife. For dessert, Heinz liked to have a small piece of pound cake and cup of coffee. I poured the coffee, put in the sugar and cream, stirred it, and then brought it over to him. Occasionally, Heinz would stare at the spoon, inspecting it carefully, to see if it was clean enough. Water stains or any kind of dirt would cause him to tell me to give him another one. It got to the point that I would just hand him a new spoon if I even saw him beginning to look at it that way.

At another meal, I cooked chicken drum sticks for the first time. I had bought a package of four drumsticks, put two aside for another night, and cooked the other two in water and made a chicken noodle soup. I had never eaten chicken before and did not know how to prepare other than boiling. When Heinz came home from work, he ate the soup and then asked what I had done with the other two drumsticks. “I saved them for another meal, Heinz.” “Well, you could have made all four of them, I was really hungry.” It had never occurred to me to serve such generous portions. I had always stretched food, and this was my way of thinking.

There was another time when I tried to make pancakes. I had never eaten them before, and I could not understand the directions on the box. I tried it and it was a disaster, they were too thin, more like crepes, and just never cooked up like pancakes. I always laughed at these blunders, too, but Heinz never laughed at any of it.

I could tell when Heinz was in a bad mood when he got home from work. The white Volkswagen door would slam, and his feet would be heavy coming towards the apartment. He would really want to eat right away. On those nights, I kept very quiet. I served him dinner and tried not to discuss anything that might upset him. Eventually, he would settle down and have a nice conversation, but I often noticed that on those nights, he would toss and turn a lot in his sleep.

I began to feel insecure because I did not believe that I was the perfect German *hausfrau* that maybe Heinz had imagined I would be. I cooked, but I didn’t really keep an immaculate house the way most German women did. I did not like to sew or knit. Maybe that is what Heinz wanted, I thought, and it made me feel bad about myself, that somehow I had not lived up to what Heinz had expected of me. I resolved to be the best wife I possibly could and I would do everything I could to make him happy. After all, he was the only family I had now.

In March, I started to feel comfortable enough to start looking for a job. Tante Else gave me a few suggestions, too. "Rubenstein Sewing Factory is looking for people," she said. Since I didn't know what else to do, I simply took her suggestion, even though I couldn't sew: I hoped they would hire me and teach me. I walked to the factory and repeated the words that Tante Else and I had practiced. "I would like to work here." After a brief interview, I was hired to sew sweaters. I really hated sewing and I was really worried if I would be able to do a good job. The boss said they would show me what I had to do. Since I really wanted this job, I just thought I would do my best and somehow I would learn what I needed to do. I started work the following Monday.

Over the weekend, Tante Else helped me buy a few dresses to wear to work. Tante Else and Onkel Fritz paid for them. "Anita, this blue dress and this brown dress are exactly what you need for work," she said confidently. I really liked the dresses, but as I looked at myself in the mirror in the store, I thought they made me look heavier than I really was. The dresses were too long, also. "*Das macht nichts*," said Tante Else, which means, that doesn't matter. "We can fix that. These are good quality dresses that will get you started for work. And you can borrow a few from my daughter, Elizabeth," she continued.

That Monday, I was nervous. "I am a little scared," I told Heinz that morning. "You know, I am really not good at sewing, I never really liked doing that sort of thing. I hope I can do a good job and they don't fire me. Do you think I look Ok this morning?" I asked him. I fussed with my hair and put on a little lipstick that Elizabeth had given me. Heinz did not like the lipstick and told me to take it off. I was so hurt. He didn't even notice how afraid I was to start this new job. I went into the bathroom and used some toilet paper to wipe off the lipstick. I dried my tears. OK, I thought, I have to pull myself together and do this on my own. I'll be OK. What is the worst thing they can do to me, fire me? So I'll just try and find another job. "Do you want me to drive you there, Anita? It's still a little cold out," asked Heinz.

"Oh, thank you Heinz, I think I would like the ride," I answered. Heinz dropped me off at the corner and wished me a good day. He kissed me good-bye and said he would look for me on the way home, and if I was walking from the trolley, he would stop and get me.

As I walked into the factory, I was first greeted by the manager who hired me. He told me I needed to fill out papers in another office. The office manager helped me and very patiently explained to me what each question meant. I turned red when asked if I was planning on applying for my US citizenship. They will not understand that everyone was forced to be in the Hitler Youth, they will hold it against me, I thought to myself. "I don't think so, not right now," I said.

After all the paperwork was done, I was shown to my seat. "Call me Jerry," said my manager. This was almost unheard of in a German workplace. An employee never called his or her boss by his first name. I learned that the factory was owned by two Jewish brothers. It was surprising to me that they would hire me, a German, who barely spoke English. There were many documentaries on television about what actually happened in Germany during the war. I was so ashamed when I watched them. I really did not want to think about it. It was too painful to believe. I was just beginning to learn the full extent about the horrible things the Nazis did to Jews in Germany, and many people seemed to distance themselves from me because I was German. Of all people, I was surprised these Jewish brothers would give me a chance, but I learned later that they hired many German people: their factory was located in a German neighborhood, and they had no prejudice towards Germans. I didn't know where they were from, but between the little bit of English that I was learning and the Yiddish that they spoke, we were basically able to communicate. I continued to hope that these two brothers would not be prejudiced against me because I was German. They did not seem to be. They were very nice to me and tried to make me comfortable. And I really liked them. They were kind to me and helped me when I was trying to speak.

I was seated next to another German lady named Paula. We immediately liked each other. Paula was from Schwarzwald, the Black Forest, which had a very distinct dialect that was also difficult to understand. My dialect was from Saxony. When local Germans spoke in their dialects, they were not able to understand each other, which is why we could communicate only in High German (the formal form of the language). Paula was a few years younger than me, with brown hair, big blue eyes, and a very kind face. She and her husband Horst were married in West Germany, but Horst had wanted to come to America to make a fresh start. Paula didn't have any family here either. She and Horst had made some friends, mostly other Germans they had met, but she too was very lonely in America. So it was nice for me to make a friend.

I was not very good with the sewing machine, but I got faster and better as time wore on. My income did help with the expenses. It was so great to have a friend. Although the job was so boring to me, my new friendship with Paula was so rich, I was so thankful. Paula and I ate lunch together every day and talked about marriage, Germany, the war, family left behind, and possible future children. To me, it was as though I had known Paula all of my life. Finding a precious friend to share life with was so important for me. I felt like I mattered to someone; like Paula understood me and accepted me just the way I was. I gladly reciprocated, and a rich lifelong friendship began to grow. She was strong, practical, loyal and loving; she became like a sister to me. We had both left behind families we loved, and we began to become family for one another.

*****

As I got to know more and more people at work and even some of the people who lived on Eleanor Street, I realized how different the American culture was from the culture I had grown up with, as a child. For example, I couldn't believe that if someone didn't like their food, they would just throw it away. One of the women in the factory had packed a bologna sandwich for lunch. She wasn't very hungry that day, so she just threw it out. I was shocked!

Also, children were freer in the way they interacted with adults. Many children called adults by their first name. That would never happen in Germany, at least not during the time that I grew up.

I was also really surprised when I saw people hanging their wash outside on Easter Sunday. That would never have happened in Germany on a Sunday, especially not Easter Sunday. It seemed to me that Americans could just do what they wanted and did not worry about what other people thought. Anticipating what people would think was an important part of how I decided what to do. I never wanted people to criticize or talk about me. Americans were not so rigid or fearful.

Also, I noticed that men treated their wives differently. For example, Mr. and Mrs. Smith invited us to join them downstairs for dinner from time to time, and I noticed they behaved more as a team: sometimes he cooked, sometimes she did, sometimes he did the dishes, sometimes she did. In German homes, the men were the boss, the king, and everyone else, including the wife, was subordinate, a lesser person. (My Papa hadn't been that way, but he was not the typical German man.) All this took some getting used to. Heinz and I built our lives on the German model since that came naturally to both of us, but as I observed other families, I realized that it did not have to be that way. Of course, I would never say anything to Heinz. He liked things just the way they were, and I was very grateful that he was taking such good care of me.

And he could be generous at times. Later that fall, I was confused when children knocked on our apartment door dressed up as ghosts, witches, and other unfamiliar characters. But Heinz knew about Halloween, and he gave them a few pennies, and then he ran to the store to buy some candy to hand out. I enjoyed seeing the children in their costumes, and I was glad Heinz and I were participating in the festivities. I liked this Halloween holiday, and I thought it was a great tradition.

Other times, though, it seemed Heinz didn't want to do much other than work. One night, Paula and Horst invited Heinz and me to visit them at their home in Fox Chase, a nice neighborhood in Philadelphia. They owned a twin home—one half of a single building divided into two homes, where two families lived separately. I was so excited about having something social to do. Heinz agreed to the plans, but when we were getting ready to go, Heinz said, "I really don't want to go now, Anita. I am so tired, and I worked so hard today." Didn't he realize how much this meant to me? My heart sank. I had been looking forward to it all day. "Ok, then Heinz, I guess I'll just call Paula and tell her you are not feeling well. I'll ask her to pick another date."

In the privacy of my thoughts, I questioned why Heinz would do this. He knew how much Paula meant to me and how much I was looking forward to this evening. Sometimes he could be so selfish, but I shouldn't think like that. Look at all he does for me. He made a way for us to come to America; he has a good job; he works so hard. I'm just not feeling that joy and freedom that I longed for when I left my homeland.

Paula graciously invited us to come the following week. This time, Heinz said he had to fix something in the car. "Ok, Heinz, we can just go a little later, I'll tell Paula." When Heinz was all done with the car, he got ready and got in the car, but there was silence the entire way there. "Did I do something wrong, Heinz?" I asked. "Oh no," came his reply, "I am just really tired, and I don't want to be there that late."

"OK, Heinz, we'll stay for a while, and then we'll just say we are tired and need to go home," I said. But when we got there, Heinz and Paula really did hit it off. Paula was a very honest and direct person, and Heinz liked that about her. The next time we went to dinner at their house, Heinz fell asleep on the sofa well before it was time to go home. I just carried on the conversation and no one said anything about it. I was a little bit embarrassed because I thought it was rude of him to fall asleep at their house, but I didn't know what else to do. I thought he fell asleep because he gets up so early to go to work and works very hard during the day. Later, I realized that he had a mild form of hypoglycemia and that there would come a time every evening when he simply could not force himself to stay awake. Our friends all came to understand that about him and it just was overlooked.

There was another time when Onkel Wilhelm and Tante Marie invited us for dinner. By the end of the night, I could not believe my ears. Heinz was arguing with Tante Marie about where a store was. She had been there and was confident of the directions, but Heinz kept insisting that she was wrong. By the end of the evening, Tante Marie was in tears. I was so humiliated by the way Heinz had treated her. I just did not know what to say or do. I just overlooked it and tried to talk about how good the meal was as we drove home. I had never confronted Heinz about his behavior, even when it embarrassed me. I also never talked about it with Tante Marie. What could I say? I didn't want to say anything bad about Heinz, but I couldn't come up with any excuse for his behavior. And Heinz was all I really had in the world. Going back to East Germany was never an option-I knew I would be immediately arrested, so I willed myself to make our marriage work.

*****

By August of 1958, I knew I was pregnant. By this time, my English had gotten a lot better, and I was confident talking to the doctor. Paula was excited, too, as she and Horst were also starting to think about a family.

One night in January of 1959, I had such a craving for cherries. I told Heinz about it, and he went all the way into center city to buy cherries at the farmers' market, since they were out of season. I think Heinz was excited about the baby, too. And I was so happy. Maybe having a baby would smooth out some of the rough spots from our first few years of married life. He really loved me and loved our baby. I hoped this would be a new beginning for us; the baby will bring back the goodness in Heinz that I fell in love with so many years ago.

Janet was born on April 9, 1959. The night I went into labor was so funny. My water broke in the middle of the night. I knew to call Dr. Rosenthal right away. He told me to go to Frankford Hospital. When I woke Heinz up and told him what was happening, he turned bright red. German men did not get into the details of "female things," and Heinz was very shy. In Germany, another woman would have been there who knew what to do, and the men could wait in another room. But since it was only the two of us, Heinz would be the only person with me, and he was uncomfortable and embarrassed that he would have to talk to the doctors. I had already packed my things, and I was very excited.

Heinz went downstairs to tell Mrs. Smith that we were leaving to go to the hospital. "My wife is leaking," he told her, meaning that my water broke. Mrs. Smith woke Mr. Smith up. "Jack, please go upstairs and see what is leaking in Heinz's apartment. Heinz seems really upset," she asked her husband. She wondered if it was the sink or the tub, and she still had trouble understanding Heinz. Even though he had been in America so much longer, my English was already better than his. Finally, Mr. Smith came back down to tell his wife what really happened, that I was in labor, that my water had broken, and that we were on the way to the hospital. Mr. and Mrs. Smith laughed about it for a long time after that. So did I, but I knew Heinz wouldn't have thought his mistake was so funny.

When Janet was born, Heinz bought me a gold ring with my birthstone, a garnet. It was really beautiful. Yet when I came home from the hospital, I saw that the dishes from our dinner from a few nights ago were still in the sink. I just cleaned everything up while Janet napped and never said anything to Heinz about it. At that point, I took maternity leave from my job.

The following week, Paula took off from work without pay to help me with the new baby. I was awfully homesick, but I was so thankful that Paula was there to learn the lessons of motherhood right along with me.

"Oh, Paula, I wish my mother were here so that she could see Janet," I said. Paula understood, and she cried along with me.

One day, Paula and I were really scared when we changed Janet's diaper. We saw something black in her diaper. We panicked. I called the pediatrician and Paula drove me. "Don't throw anything away: I want to see what you are talking about," said Dr. Cohen.

When Dr. Cohen saw Janet, the black thing, and the diaper, he knew that the umbilical cord had fallen off, exactly as it was supposed to. Paula and I laughed. Paula was glad to know this: she and I were both learning together. That night, after Paula went home, I told Heinz about the incident. "Oh, Heinz, we were so embarrassed, and we just started laughing. Dr. Cohen probably thinks I have no idea what I am doing. But I guess that is how mothers learn," I said. Heinz didn't say anything. "Are you mad, Heinz?" Heinz never answered me, and I then realized that he had been terribly embarrassed by my blunder and didn't want to talk about it anymore.

A few days later, Janet had a fever and I called the doctor for a recipe. "What do you mean?" asked the doctor.

"My daughter has a fever, and I need a recipe for the drug store to bring her fever down." After much guffawing, the doctor finally realized that I was talking about a prescription: in German, *recipe* and *prescription* are the same word because many doctors were homeopaths and would give families instructions on how to prepare a medicine. I laughed at all these blunders, and I had fun telling the neighbors and Mrs. Smith all about it. Plus, I was thrilled to learn another English word. When Heinz came home from work that night, I told him the whole story. "You should learn English better, Anita," was all he said. My English was much better than his was, and I enjoyed learning new words, but I said nothing. I always avoided any conflict with him.

The next day Mrs. Smith knocked on my door and I invited her in for a visit. "Anita, I will help you any time," said Mrs. Smith. And she did. Mrs. Smith often went to the store and bought groceries for us so I would not have to take Janet out of the apartment. Mrs. Smith came over during the day and checked on me to see if I was Ok.

"Anita, I had 10 children. Call me anytime," she said.

I was so grateful for her: I missed my Mama so much while I was pregnant and now that Janet was born, I missed her even more. Mrs. Smith knew how homesick I was for my family in Germany. Her own children were grown and out of the house, and she seemed to be "adopting" us, which I so appreciated.

When my maternity leave ended, I tried going back to the sewing factory in the evenings. But Heinz really did not want to take care of Janet by himself, and Heinz did not want to ask his aunts for help, so we decided it was best for me to give up the job at the sewing factory. I thought it was too bad that Heinz couldn't take care of the baby just for a few hours, and we could certainly have used the extra money my job would have brought in, but I said nothing to Heinz. Instead, I accepted my new role as a mother, and I enjoyed taking care of my new baby girl. I hoped we would have more children as well.

*****

"Every good and perfect gift is from above coming down from the Father of heavenly lights, who does not change like shifting shadows." James 1:17

—8—

Having Children Filled My Heart with Happiness

In June of 1960, two years later, Heinz and I bought a house in northeast Philadelphia at 9912 Medway Road. It cost $12,000, and it was new construction. It was a very nice Irish Catholic neighborhood at the very outskirts of the city, not too far from Fox Chase, where Paula and Horst lived. The home was a twin home with three bedrooms and one full bathroom and one toilet in the basement. There was an eat-in kitchen that was in the front of the house, so from the kitchen window, I could look outside to watch for Heinz, and later for the children. The kitchen led into the dining room, and that room led into the living room. It was open so that if we had a party, everyone in the living room and dining room could see each other. The front of the house had white stucco and green shutters.

At the end of the driveway, there was a garage. That was perfect for Heinz: he could keep all his tools in there. The back door of the basement led to a patio and a really nice backyard. We fenced it in with a chain link fence. To me, it was a mansion. I felt terrible when I thought of the way my family was living. Multiple families sometimes had to share apartments in East Germany. Renate and her husband had a daughter, Marion, and they just had a curtain separating her bedroom area from their own. Renate shared her kitchen and bathroom with another family.

What I loved most about our new house was that the yard backed up to fields and then woods. The rest of the streets in the neighborhood had houses in front and back of them, but Medway Road was at the top of the neighborhood, with electric company land behind. The backyard was so nice. When we moved in, Heinz immediately started a vegetable garden and planted two peach trees and one apple tree.

"I am never going to starve like we did during and after the war," he said. I was very grateful that I was in America. I felt so fortunate to even own a house. Who would have ever thought that we would have a whole house with eight rooms and enough land to plant our own garden for just the three of us?

A year after we moved into the house, Carol was born; Robert followed close behind the next year. When Carol was born, we were a little short on money, so Heinz only bought me flowers. The following year, Heinz bought me a stereo to celebrate Robert's birth. He knew how much I would enjoy it, even though he was not interested in music at all.

As a young child, Janet was very blonde with blue eyes. Eventually, her hair got darker as she got older. She did not really look like either one of us. Carol had brown hair and blue eyes, but she was very petite, with very delicate features, and I always thought that she looked a lot like my Mama. Robert also had brown hair and hazel eyes, and when I looked at him, he reminded me of my brother Karli.

By the time we were married five years, we had a house with a yard and three preschool children. My dreams were coming true. I was so happy to be able to raise my children in a free country where our hard work paid off and we could live with dignity. Being a mother was one of the greatest joys of my life. Paula had a son named Jeffrey who was born the same year as Carol. We got together with Paula all the time since Paula had stopped working after Jeffrey was born. We played hide and go seek and tag in our backyard together. One of the things I loved to do was to have the children gather around me and I would tell them a story. Sometimes I told them fairy tales that we learned in Germany and sometimes I made up stories that I thought they would enjoy. I just loved seeing the expressions on their faces as they imagined themselves in the story. One of those stories became a family favorite at Easter time. The children, especially Janet, would ask me to tell the story of "Fuzzytail" over and over again. Fuzzytail was about the littlest bunny in the Easter bunny family who was too small to hold the paintbrush and decorate the Easter eggs the way the others could. Instead, he just struggled to lift the brush and put a dot on the egg. That was my imagined story of where the speckled Easter eggs came from. When my grandchildren were born, I wrote down the story so their mothers could read the same story them.[4] Family traditions were so important to me.

Those were joyful years, and I felt fulfilled. Our home was like a bubbling brook: everyone talked at the same time. Since all three kids were close in age, they competed for my attention. It was wonderful, except I always wished my Mama would have been around to help me, too. At least I had Paula.

Heinz put up dark paneling in the basement a few years later so the kids could have a playroom down there. He built shelves for storage under the steps. I felt like we were building a good life together.

But not long after we moved in, we discovered that someone had painted a swastika on our garage. When Heinz got up for work one morning, he saw it and then had to paint over it before he went to work. I was so hurt by this act. But then it made me think about Kristallnacht and how the Jewish people had been treated in Germany by the Nazis. I felt ashamed all over again as I pondered the dark actions of my countrymen.

But the swastika appeared again a few weeks later. And again. Heinz painted over it every time, and I just died a little bit inside. I just wanted to put the whole ordeal of the war behind me. We never knew who was doing this, but it was very frightening to wonder who in our neighborhood might be against us. I was always friendly and good to all of the neighbors, but I could never completely trust anyone.

One neighbor, Sylvia, lived a few houses apart from us. No one really embraced her when she first moved in because she was Jewish, but at least her property was not vandalized by anyone. Since we were both outcasts, Sylvia and I became very friendly. We laughed about the irony that we had become good friends, a German and a Jew, amidst Irish Catholic Americans. Sylvia was the first Jewish person I really got to know as a friend. I just couldn't understand why the Nazis had so much against Jewish people. She loved her family, was a good neighbor, and a hard worker, and she did her best to do what was right.

Prejudice is a very strange thing. It occurs when there is a majority of one kind and a minority of another kind. It never has anything to do with actually knowing the people involved. Unfortunately, prejudice is often taught to people, especially children. Just like when I used to see the signs that falsely stated that the Jews wanted the war. When I first came to America and saw all the different nationalities represented here, I thought there was a great deal of tolerance. But I soon realized that there is prejudice everywhere. That is why Germans moved into the same section of Philadelphia, the Feltonville section. Italians lived together in certain sections of Philadelphia, and Hispanics, too. No one ever wants to feel different or be an outcast.

Almost all of the children in the neighborhood went to parochial school, but my kids and Sylvia's children went to public school. Fortunately, the initial prejudice that we experienced when we first moved in died out soon enough. Eventually, we became very friendly with all of the neighbors. I tried my best to get along with everyone. But I was always cautious that because we were German, people might still be prejudiced against us. Heinz was different. He came home from work and stayed in the house. He was not interested in making friends with the neighbors. He never fully trusted them. Later on, though, he did get friendly with some of the neighbors who liked to play pinochle. They often played cards on the weekends. But that was after we had already lived there for more than ten years.

I also encouraged my children to make friends with all types of people. Many of Carol's schoolmates, for example, had immigrant parents from many countries: India, Hungary, the Ukraine, to name just a few. She learned a little about each of her friends' traditional customs. She had become especially friendly with a girl named Debbie, who wore glasses, and she had very long brown hair. Carol told me she thought Debbie looked a bit like her sister, Janet.

Debbie and Carol had become very good friends: they went to each other's homes all the time. Debbie even invited Carol to a Passover Seder meal at her Aunt Naomi's house in Ventnor, New Jersey. Carol told me that Debbie had warned her, on the way over in the car with her family, not to eat the Gefilte fish: "It is disgusting,"

Debbie said, "No one ever eats it. Just take your fork and twirl it around like you do with pasta. Spread the fish around the plate and my aunt won't realize that you did not eat any. I don't know why my Aunt Naomi even bothers getting it each year." Carol told me later how relieved she was that Debbie had forewarned her because when she saw it, she thought it looked disgusting, too.

When Carol got home, she told me all about the gefilte fish, but she also said she liked some of the other food, especially matzoth (which I had never heard of), and she enjoyed learning about the Passover Seder. She thought it was so funny that they put a glass of wine out for Elijah, the Old Testament prophet whom the Jews expect for Passover every year.

Debbie's family was always so kind to Carol; she told me even Debbie's grandfather always made her feel welcome. They called him *zaydeh,* which is the Jewish word for grandfather, and every time Carol visited, he bought expensive cheesecake because he knew how much she liked it. Since Debbie was Jewish, she had never made Christmas cookies, and Carol thought it would be fun, so she asked if she could invite Debbie her over to do that with me and Janet. I had my Mama's recipe for butter cookies, which reminded me of Christmases in Germany: I missed my Mama and Papa and sisters and brothers, but making these cookies with my daughters and their friends made the holidays sweeter for all of us. We used a cookie press to make different shapes: Christmas trees, stars, Santa, and even dogs. I made sure we had plenty of jimmies, sprinkles, chocolate chips, and red and green sugar, to decorate the cookies. Debbie and Carol also made their own designs with the little bit of remaining batter.

It was fun for me to watch the girls playing with the cookie dough, and after we had cleaned up, I told Debbie she should take home as many of the cookies as she wanted, since her family didn't make Christmas cookies, of course. I knew the cookies would be delicious because my Mama's recipe was wonderful, and I wanted Debbie's family to know how much I liked that she and Carol were friends. I was insecure around Debbie, but I never told Carol that. I wanted Carol's Jewish friends to know that Germans could be nice, too.

By now, I had been in America long enough to understand just how clever and evil the Nazi manipulation had been. WWII documentaries continued to air on television. I did not want to watch them anymore. I wanted to have pride in my country and didn't want to dwell on the evil. But it seemed like everyone was obsessed with it. Because of that, I was afraid to apply for U.S. citizenship. I would have been granted it, since Heinz was a citizen and I was his spouse, but I feared the prejudice and worried that because I had been part of the Hitler youth that they might hold that against me. I felt inferior and was not sure if I was really good enough to be a U.S. citizen.

Another thing that shocked me was how people in America were willing to discuss politics. People freely criticized the mayor of Philadelphia when the snow was not removed from the streets quickly enough. Most people liked President Kennedy, but occasionally I would overhear critical comments from one of the neighbors. This was something that never happened when I grew up. People were afraid to speak out against the establishment.

*****

I loved having three children and was determined to teach them German, the German culture, and all of the traditions from my homeland. There was so much more to the German people than the Nazi's and the war. It was important for me to teach my children about the wonderful heritage they had in their German ancestry. I really wanted my children to speak both German and English, so I would sit them down at the kitchen table and hold up various objects. "Knife, *messer*," I would say. Then I would just say one of the words and whatever child I was working with had to say the other word. "Plate," I would say. Then Janet would answer "*Teller*." Janet learned to speak German fluently, but Carol refused to speak German, I think because she was embarrassed when she went to school and got confused between the two languages.

When Carol was in kindergarten, her teacher asked the class to cut out pictures for a particular letter of the alphabet that they worked on each week, I suppose to help them learn to read and write. When they got to the letter "H," I helped Carol cut out a picture of a hamper from a magazine. The German word for hamper is *Waeschekorb*, and Carol was more accustomed to using the German word than the English word, *hamper,* which she had not really learned yet. I knew that Carol had trouble with this word, so I reminded her several times on the morning the project was due, to make sure she knew the word was *hamper.*

I also knew that Carol didn't like her kindergarten teacher: she thought her teacher was 'an old hag' (which is how she describes her today; at the time, I believe she used the word 'witch') because she said her teacher intimidated all the children in the class. As Carol described her, her teacher was around fifty years old, had spaces missing between her teeth, and she sounded like she was gargling all the time. Carol told me she was not really the type of person that children should have as their first teacher. So I was worried for Carol on this particular day, hoping she wouldn't have problems remembering the English word, *hamper.* Unfortunately, my worries were realized, when Carol came home in tears and told me what had happened at school.

Carol's teacher went around to each child and asked each what his or her picture was. When she got to Carol, my daughter told me she just couldn't think clearly: she had forgotten the word for hamper, and she blurted out *Waeschekorb*. And the teacher reacted badly: instead of gently correcting her, or even sternly correcting my sweet little girl, the teacher ripped out the picture that she had so carefully glued into her large brown scrapbook and held it up in Carol's face. Then the teacher made fun of Carol by taunting, "If this is a *Waeschekorb*, then it should go under the letter *"V!"* and she sprayed saliva across Carol's desk as she said it. Carol was so mortified that she did not say anything at the time, but when she came home from school that day, she told me all about what happened.

When she showed me her torn scrapbook, I just started to cry. I knew how difficult it is to learn a new language, but I was an adult when I came to the United States, and it didn't bother me when I made mistakes. In fact, it usually made me laugh at myself, like the time I was in the maternity section of the department store before I was even married because I didn't know what the sign said, or the time Heinz tried to tell our landlord that my water had broken but instead they thought something was leaking in our apartment.

Those mistakes seemed funny to me, though I also remembered when I was trying to learn English in night school with other immigrants, who all laughed at my terrible pronunciation and my heavy German accent. So I could see how my 5-year-old daughter would feel humiliated by her teacher's mockery in front of all her classmates. I realized Carol just wanted to be a 'normal' kid who knew the right English words for things, so I wasn't surprised when she began to reject the German language and refuse to learn it or speak it.

Then when Robert learned to talk, he began to stutter very badly, because he could not handle learning both languages all mixed together. Since then, I learned that for children to learn two languages one parent needs to speak one language and the other parent needs to speak the other language. Otherwise, the child does not learn which words go together in a language. Robert stuttered when he first started to speak – I think it was because he knew two words for everything and didn't know which one to pick.

When Heinz saw what was happening, he decided, "Well, we are living here, we have to just talk English to the kids, so they will be OK. We'll just talk German to each other." By this time, my English was so much better than Heinz's. Even though I was home with the children, I interacted with people, the neighbors, the children's friends, and store personnel all the time. When Heinz and I spoke to each other, it was about 80% German and 20% English. With the kids, although I tried my best to speak only English, I usually still put one or two German words in the sentence, whichever word came to my mind first. Carol was so adamant about not speaking German that if I used even one German word in an otherwise completely English sentence, she would ask me to repeat the entire sentence with the correct English word. It helped me learn English faster, that much is for sure. And I understood why she was so determined not to speak or even listen to German.

*****

Even though Carol didn't want to learn German and Robert had difficulty, I still wanted all of my kids to experience the German traditions that I had loved when I was a child. At Christmastime, we celebrated the four advents. We lit candles, and I taught them the German Advent song. Translating into English, it goes somewhat like this:

"Now we light the first candle on this green Christmas wreath.

So with its sparking light, the Christmas season celebration can begin."

Then on Saint Nicholas Day, which is December 6th, I put chocolate in the children's shoes.

Also, at the beginning of every Christmas season, we bought German advent calendars from a German butcher. These calendars are for children. For each day in December, a child opens a rectangular or square door on the calendar. The calendar has a Christmas scene on it, usually of Santa Claus and his reindeer. Behind each numbered door, there is a piece of chocolate. The last day on the calendar is December 24th, when Germans celebrate Christmas. I always celebrated that way with my family. I wanted my children to celebrate Christmas this way also, so we always opened our gifts on Christmas Eve.

I wanted to give my children a sense of family, especially because we did not have much family in the United States: Heinz's brothers Fritz and Wilhelm both died when our children were very young, and Carol has no memory of them at all. Fortunately, we were blessed to have wonderful friends who were also German-Americans: not only Paula, who I had met at the sewing factory and her husband Horst, but also Günter and Elfriede, and John and Theresa. Heinz had met Günter in the army (during the Korean War), and John had been a neighbor when Heinz was single and living in an apartment building. These men and their wives became surrogate uncles and aunts for Janet, Carol, and Robert: they even called them *Onkel* and *Tante*.

We usually spent Christmas Eve with Günter and Elfriede: Günter dressed up as Santa Claus to deliver the gifts to the kids in person on Christmas Eve. I had told our children about Santa Claus, who in Germany is called *the Weinachtsmann* in German, but as they got older, they began to question whether he was real. I wanted the kids to cling to the fantasy for as long as possible, but Carol got so frustrated one year, and she finally asked Heinz, who told her, "No, Carol, there really is no such thing as Santa Claus." I was disappointed, but Carol was very grateful that her father had told her the truth.

Also at Christmastime, Renate coordinated among my family members and sent one big package of gifts for us. She usually sent hand-crafted wooden items from the Erzgebirge region in Saxony. I really loved those hand-made wooden crafts that were produced in the Erzgebirge. One year, Renate sent a tall white *pyramide*, a traditional Christmas decoration that is made there and usually exported, but she was able to get this one. The pyramide was about 18 inches high, with three tiers. On the bottom was a hand-carved manger scene and candle holders. The second tier had the three wise men, also hand carved. The third tier had delicately carved angels that hung from the top with metal fasteners. The angels were still in the natural wood, while the wise men and the manger scene were painted with different colors. There were also clear glass bells on the top of the *pyramide*. The very top has wings or fans of wood that are tilted at an angle. When the candles from the first tier are lit, heat rises, and the three tiers spin.

Nutcrackers are hand-made in the Erzgebirge too, as are the Bergman (mountain man) figures. The mountain men are usually painted a bright green, and they always wear a hat. Sometimes they are made in two pieces, a top half and a bottom half. Then a piece of incense can be placed in the bottom half. When lit, the smoke comes out of the Bergman's mouth. Over the years, Renate sent all these items, and I always displayed them at Christmastime.

I always sent packages to my family and Heinz's family too. I often bought clothes for all of our nieces and nephews over there. We tried to send special food items, but they were usually removed from the packages before they got to our family members. One year when my brother Karli was eight, I sent him a pair of pants, and I put a can of sardines inside one of the pockets. He loved sardines. I always wrote to my Mama ahead of time and told her exactly what was in the package. The pants came, but the sardines were taken out. Probably the person who opened the package took it home to his family that day. I also tried to send good chocolate one year, but that never made it either. When my children outgrew their clothing, if the items were still in good condition, I sent those clothes over for the younger cousins to use, because good-quality clothing was still not always available to purchase in East Germany.

I always loved Christmastime, but the Christmas of 1966 was especially nice. That Christmas Eve, the three children were told to wait upstairs while Santa delivered the gifts. That year, Heinz had made natural wood-colored cribs for Janet's and Carol's dolls. The cribs were about a foot long. They had curved bottoms so the girls could pretend to be rocking their dolls back and forth. He had painted a pink rose on the inside headboard of each crib. Since I knew he was making those, I bought two new Teeny Weenie Tiny Tears dolls and some cloth to use as blankets for them. Heinz had also made a set of wooden soldiers for Robert.

He also spent a few weeks in the garage working on a playhouse for all three children. He put it in the backyard when it was finished and took everyone outside that night on Christmas Eve so the children could see it right away. The playhouse was the size of a shed, with a roof. Heinz had painted it white and cut out sections and smoothed those surfaces for windows. He glued extra carpet scraps to the floor. Heinz also made wooden benches for the inside. The children were so excited when they saw it. We enjoyed it for many years, and so did the neighborhood children. Eventually, though, some of the neighborhood children began to leave trash in it, and a few times, some of the boys urinated in it. Heinz was hurt, so he just burned it down.

*****

I also wanted my children to know German traditions in their everyday lives, not only at Christmastime. So on Sundays, I always made a hot meal to eat at noon (called *Mittagessen*, or mid-day meal). In Germany, this dinner-type meal is eaten at lunch time, and in the evening, most people have bread and cold cuts. So on Sundays, I always did this with our family. The noon meal was always followed by a walk in the woods and then a nice Sunday afternoon nap. Sundays were always days where we celebrated special family times. Sometimes we would get up early and take a drive into the country or go sightseeing as a family. Heinz loved having his kids with him, and he loved showing them things – as long as they behaved.

Heinz really enjoyed the kids when they were little. When he got home from work, he played ball with them in the backyard. In the winter, they went sledding with him in the hills and fields right outside of our backyard.

One night, Heinz stayed in the garage and worked on something. I had no idea what he was doing and did not ask him. After a few nights of this, Heinz walked up to the living room through the basement with an oval Formica table about three feet long. The table had very short legs.

"I made this for the kids, Anita. They kept hitting their head on the corners of the other table, so I will put that one in the garage and the kids can use this one. I made it from scraps that I had left over from work." His smile was as wide as the table.

*****

I marveled at how the children in the neighborhood were so free, in how they acted and in their speech and attitudes. Children in the neighborhood never hesitated to knock on our door if a ball went into our backyard. Parents would fight with the teachers if their children got bad grades and would often demand that their child be allowed to be re-tested. That would have never happened in Germany. In the culture of Germany during my childhood, authority was never questioned. No one would have dreamed of confronting a teacher about anything for their child.

Of course, not questioning authority is not always a good thing, as evidenced by the horrors wrought by the Nazis. As much as I wanted to introduce my children to the wonderful German traditions of my childhood, I also wanted to protect my children from knowing about Nazi Germany. I felt they were too young to understand, and I didn't want them to experience the same prejudice I felt when people called me a Nazi or painted swastikas on our garage.

But no parent can protect her children forever, and sure enough, when Carol was in elementary school, some boy yelled "Nazis" to her and Robert as they were getting off the bus. They had never even heard this word before, so when they arrived home, they asked me what it meant. I felt sick. I didn't want to tell her: after all, she was only about 10 years old and Robert was only 9. So I just said, "Oh that is a very bad thing, a bad word. Just don't even talk about it."

Carol was always persistent, though, and when Heinz came home from work, she asked him about it as he sat on his chair to read the paper. And Heinz told her the truth. Carol then talked to Janet, who already knew about the Nazis from school. Carol was furious: she screamed to Janet, "HOW COULD OUR MOTHER NOT TELL ME SOMETHING LIKE THAT?" Janet promised to get some books out of the library for Carol, so she could read more about it—about what Carol called 'Germany's REAL history.'

Then at dinner a few weeks later, Carol again asked us about what she had learned. Carol sat on the left side of the table since she is left-handed and she sat next to Heinz. She looked right at Heinz when she asked her questions.

"Unfortunately, all of it is true," said Heinz sadly.

"All of our friends from school are Jewish. They are our best friends. Their families are so nice to me! I cannot believe you never told us this happened in Germany," Carol said to both of us. I could see how angry she was, but now she was looking at me. I knew she thought I had betrayed her somehow.

"Yes, it happened in Germany. It was a very bad time in Germany," said Heinz again. He was very serious. And although I agreed with him, I remember saying emphatically, "I just want to forget all about it now and put it behind me. That was a terrible war and a terrible time. Gypsies and people who did not agree with the government were also put in those concentration camps. But I just do not want to think about it anymore." And I got up from the table and began to do the dishes and hoped that Carol would just drop it.

*****

For the most part, those years when my three children were so young were very enjoyable for me: I just didn't want anything to get in the way of how happy I was with them. I loved being a mother. I always wished that my Mama would have been able to see my children grow up. I also wished that I could call her once in a while, but that was not possible. Most East Germans still did not have phones, and even if they did, they would not have been allowed to call outside of the communist block of countries. I guess because I was always so lonely for my family, I would often ask Heinz, "Can't you just tell me that you love me?" And he would say, "Well Anita, you know everything already anyway."

I still talked about missing my Mama all the time and how much I wished she could meet our children. Heinz realized it and started working some overtime to earn the money for my Mama to come to America for a visit. About a year later, Heinz thought he had earned enough. As we sat down at breakfast together before he went to work, he said, "Write to your Mama to make sure she has a passport, and then we can get Tante Else's sister, Tante Ida in West Germany, to help her make the arrangements."

I had never met Tante Ida before, but Tante Else had always said that her sister would help our family in East Germany if we ever needed her. The East German government allowed anyone who was on *Rente* (which is the equivalent of Social Security or a pension) to travel to West Germany. If they didn't come back, the government wouldn't have to pay their pension anymore, so anyone over 65 was always granted permission to go. My Mama had gotten permission to go to West Germany only. The East German government was not aware that she would be going to the United States. But Tante Ida had arranged it all.

The entire family went to New York to meet my Mama at the airport. She arrived in October 1969. Heinz looked ahead through the lines and saw her. "She is here, Anita," he said.

I just gasped, "Are you sure she is here, Heinz?" I was afraid to believe it.

"Yes, I saw her," Heinz said with a big smile.

It had been thirteen years since I had seen my Mama, since she came to Oberhausen, when Heinz and I thought we could get married in West Germany. Since that time, my parents had gotten divorced (in 1962), and I did not want to talk about that. I could not accept it. To me, they were still married, and when I thought of home, it all needed to be intact. Both of my parents were precious to me and it was unthinkable to me that they could not work out their differences. I did not talk about my parents' divorce to anyone for many years.

When my Mama came through the doorway into the waiting area, I just bawled uncontrollably. She and I hugged, and I couldn't stop crying. I introduced my Mama to my children, who were seeing their grandmother for the first time. Janet was 10, Carol 8, and Robert 7. My children spoke enough German, Janet was the best, but everyone was able to converse with her.

It was a wonderful month for me. During her stay, we took her to the Jersey shore, to New York, to the Poconos, and all throughout the city of Philadelphia. My Mama enjoyed watching the family shows on television, even though she could not understand anything. She watched *The Brady Bunch* and *My Three Sons*. Every time my Mama went to the supermarket with us, she wanted to buy everything right away.

"You better buy the eggs and deodorant now, Anita. You may not be able to get them again for another month," she said.

We tried to convince her that we would be able to buy everything again the next day, but she just could not believe it. It made me wonder just how bad things really were in East Germany.

When Halloween came, Carol dressed up as a princess, Robert was an army soldier, and Janet was a doctor. My mama thought the holiday was so much fun. After a few kids came to the door in their costumes, my Mama wanted to be the one to put the candy in their pumpkins or bags. At that time, there were close to a hundred children who came to our door on Halloween. My Mama loved it.

When it was time to take her back, Heinz and I drove her to the airport by ourselves. It was so sad for me to see her go again. "Thank you, Heinz, for working extra all those months to pay for my mother's trip. It meant so much, you will never know," I said to him after my Mama left.

"*Ach,* Anita, I am glad that you enjoyed the time with her," he said. He enjoyed having her with us, too.

I continued to write long letters to each of my siblings and parents each month. I especially wanted my Mama to continue to feel like she knew her grandchildren. Lots of pictures were always included with the letters. She wrote to me every week. Below is one letter that my Mama wrote to me a few years after she had been in America.

31.3.71 Gertrude to Anita

To my children,

Now I have no peace anymore because every day when I come from work, every day I go to the mailbox and hope there would be a letter from you. I hope that you are not all sick with the flu because you, my dear Anita, mentioned in your last letter that there is an epidemic where you live. And when I do not get any mail, then I worry. If it should have happened, then I hope that all of you got through this OK. For you, Janet, I am going to send a little present for your birthday in April. It is so terrible that so many things are not allowed to be sent. There are so many beautiful things, a little skirt, but you cannot send anything, shoes, nothing is allowed.

Marion [Renate's daughter] wants to become a nurse. She is doing very well. Say hello to all your friends to me. Heartfelt greetings from me. Oh, my left hand is itching so much, it is itching so much; I think I am going to get this long-awaited mail by tomorrow. Did you get the letter from Karli?

I wanted so desperately to maintain those relationships with my Mama, Papa, and siblings. I was still very lonely in the United States. Nothing ever replaces having your real family there. Heinz just could not or would not meet my emotional needs. I kept burying the way I really felt, pretended I was happy and put all my energy into trying to make a good home for my children.

*****

"If you, then, though you are evil, know how to give good gifts to your children, how much more will your Father in heaven give good gifts to those who ask him!" Matthew 7:11

—9—

Becoming a U.S. Citizen

In 1970, when I was 38 years old, I got brave enough to apply for my U.S. citizenship. I had no trouble and enjoyed learning about the Constitution, the Declaration of Independence, and the Bill of Rights. The neighbors talked me into having a party to celebrate. It did not take much coaxing and I agreed. I invited the neighbors and some of our friends over to our house. I made all the food and it was really fun. Everyone bought gifts, which really surprised me. I got red, white, and blue drinking glasses; red, white, and blue towels, and an American flag. Some of the neighbors even gave me money. One neighbor bought me a red, white, and blue pin. Another gave me a red, white, and blue scarf. I couldn't believe it. I was very proud.

I had also learned to drive, but I was always nervous in the car. Before Janet's 13th birthday, I had nightmares that something awful was going to happen. Sometimes, I woke up and was covered with sweat, and I knew I had some terrible dream about her, that something horrific was going to happen. It was shrugged off, but the nightmare often returned.

In 1972, Janet's confirmation and her 13th birthday fell around the same time. Naturally, we decided to have a party after the ceremony and we invited a few of her friends, some from school and one girl from the neighborhood. Previously, Heinz and I had joined the German club that offered German choir (for me) and other social activities. We met many of our German friends there, too. So we decided to go there for dinner to celebrate Janet's special day. On the way home from the German club, I was driving one of our cars with Janet, Carol, and three of Janet's friends in the back seat. We were only five minutes away from our home, when we were driving down a steep hill and the brakes failed. I felt so responsible—there were five children in that car with me. Pumping the brakes did not work either. My heart began to race. The children were all frightened, they could see what was happening, but no one said a word. I kept pumping the brakes, and eventually they began to slow the car. At the bottom of the hill, I saw a gas station and pulled into the lot. I then used the emergency brake to bring the car to a complete stop. All the color was gone from my face, I am sure. I was shaking. The girls assured me they were all OK.

From the gas station, we called Mr. Cella, one of our neighbors and the father of one of Janet's friends. He came to get us and drove us home. After that, the day was over for me. The thought that something could have happened to any one of those children while they were in the car with me was just unbearable. Heinz came home with Robert a while later. He could not understand what happened, since the car had just been inspected. “Ach, Anita, everyone is OK. I do not understand why you are still so upset,” he said. Heinz did not understand at all.

After that incident, my uneasiness about driving became worry, fear, and anxiety behind the wheel. I drove because the children needed me to get them to friends, after- school functions, and to the store, but I was always filled with dread. Whenever I was in the middle of a large intersection, about to make a left turn, I felt panic, and I would then breathe an enormous sigh of relief once I had made that turn. I began to drive different ways, just to avoid left turns, if possible.

A few months after Janet’s 13th birthday, there was another driving incident. Heinz and I had taken both cars out so he could drop one off to get inspected. As we were driving, I had a sort of panic attack. I lost all feeling in my legs. It felt like there were daggers in my chest. I could no longer drive, so I somehow pulled the car over to the side of the road and hoped that Heinz realized I was no longer behind him. Fortunately, he did see what was happening. We were already right near the car dealer, so once Heinz dropped off his car, he walked back over to me. I was still sitting in the car. I could not move my legs at all. My hands were shaking. I felt light-headed. Cold sweat covered my face, neck, and arms. Heinz took me to the nearest hospital. After being there for quite some time, the doctors explained that I had suffered an anxiety attack.

After that, I really almost never drove. Once in a while, I drove down the hill in our neighborhood, parked the car, and crossed the main road by foot to buy a few items from a local quick mart. But I would never leave the development and drive onto a main road. Heinz could not understand my anxiety, but there was nothing he could do or say to change it either.

After the driving incidences and the lack of sympathy that Heinz showed, I realized that he was never going to support me emotionally. He only criticized me. My own emotional strength was failing: I was now suffering from uncontrolled anxiety. Despite having three wonderful children that gave me a lot of joy, I still felt very alone.

*****

"But whoever listens to me will live in safety, and be at ease, without fear or harm." Proverbs 1:33

—10—

Heinz Was Never Happy

I often thought back to my own childhood, about how I had loved my Papa so much: I loved his musical talent and his natural warmth and goodness. But I also knew that he had difficulty providing for our family, financially, and that was what had caused strife in our household, between my Papa and my Mama. That's also what led my Mama to divorce him eventually. And I believe the financial strain of my childhood is what led me to marry Heinz, whom I knew was hardworking and ambitious and would be a good provider for me and our children in our new home. I believe that's also what led both of my sisters, Renate and Erika, to marry the men they married—men who are very pragmatic and stable. I can't comment on their marriages, but I know my own was difficult because I didn't feel loved by Heinz—and neither did my children.

Heinz would often lecture the children about people who lived above their means. "We as a family will never do that," he often said. Every once in a while, we would take a ride to Philadelphia on a Saturday morning and drive through dilapidated neighborhoods of row homes. The kids had no idea where we were, but the purpose of the drive was clear enough: Heinz often said, "Take a look at these unfortunate people. Look at their damaged homes. Do you see the missing windows? Can you see that they do not have a backyard to play in? You kids should be so grateful that you have a home and a nice backyard to play in." These weren't pleasant conversations; it was more like a lecture, and the children were a captive audience, trapped by their seat belts in the backseat of our car. They never answered Heinz, of course; they just listened and hoped the drive would be over soon.

As did I. Although I tried to distract Heinz from these poverty lectures by commenting on what a pretty day it was, or by pointing our various flowers or trees, he was undeterred from his goal of making our children realize how much better their lives were than our own had been. In my efforts to be a "good German wife," I admit I wasn't comfortable enough to let him know how intimidated the children were by these lectures.

I kept hoping that the man I fell in love with would return. He was the father that I wanted for my children, not the man I was now living with who was obsessed with the finances. When the "Jack and Jill" ice cream truck rolled into the neighborhood in the summer, the kids never even bothered to ask their father for any money. They would hear the little song and the bell from the truck, but they didn't even go outside; they just watched from our kitchen window as the other neighborhood children, like flies to honey, descended on the truck and got in line to buy their ice cream. One time, one of our neighbors, Mr. O'Hara, asked Heinz, "Why don't you just buy your kids an ice cream cone once in a while?" Heinz answered emphatically: "It is the principle of the matter. These kids need to learn how easy it is to fall into poverty. One day, we may not have enough money. Then we will be sorry we wasted it on overpriced ice cream from a truck. Things can change quickly. That's what happened to us in Germany. I remember starving. I won't ever let that happen again, if I have anything to do with it."

Here, at least, I could change things: when I started to work, and I had some money of my own, I gave it to the children so they could buy an ice cream from the truck. When the kids were older, I worked part-time at various jobs: in the kitchen of our German club, in the kitchen of a local luncheonette that I could walk to, and in the lunchroom at Carol's middle school. But when the kids were very young and I wasn't working, I had to respect my husband's decisions about how our money could be spent.

Because he didn't want to "waste" any money, we went to the New Jersey shore in the summer for only a single day, instead of going for a few days or even a week. Heinz insisted on getting the kids up at 6AM and packing them in the car so we could be on the beach by 9AM, and I packed sandwiches and drinks for lunch, though occasionally Heinz would let the kids buy hot dogs or hamburgers on the boardwalk. On the way down and back, Heinz wanted silence, so he often told the kids, "Let's see who can be quietest in the car all the way down to the shore." Fortunately, that was not really a problem for them because they were still so tired from getting up so early. Afterwards, the kids were allowed to ride the small roller coaster, the merry-go-round, and the bumper cars before it was time to go home. They did enjoy the rides, but this one day at the beach was hardly a vacation.

Heinz also seemed to enjoy teasing the children, which I didn't understand. If we did not eat dinner on the boardwalk, as we got close to home, he usually asked the kids if they wanted to eat at McDonald's. Of course, this was a treat, because we almost never ate out, and McDonald's had just come to our neighborhood and was still something of a novelty, though even back then, kids loved their food. Janet, Carol, and Robert would answer almost in unison, "Yes, we want to eat at McDonalds!" They were so excited. Heinz would drive right up to the restaurant, and then he would pull out of the parking lot and say to me, "No, Anita, you can just make scrambled eggs for the kids when we get home." I knew our kids were confused and disappointed, but they never got angry or argued with their father when this happened; they just kept quiet, and looked straight ahead. I wanted to argue with him, but I never did.

It sounds like a trivial incident, but I realized then that at some point, we had all become afraid to argue with Heinz. That only made matters worse. He would have lectured the kids about how lucky they were to be living in a nice house, which was so much better than Heinz's own childhood home. I knew Heinz had had a difficult childhood, because his mother had left him as a baby and he had lived his first 6 years with his grandparents. But when his father married Marta, they raised him in their home, with his half-sister and half-brother. I had met Heinz's father and stepmother, and I saw how much they cared for him. So I didn't understand why he enjoyed taunting our own kids this way.

But as the kids got older, Heinz became even more ridiculous. He came home from work one day and installed a toothpaste dispenser by mounting it to the pale green tiled wall in our bathroom. The toothpaste tube hung upside down on the dispenser, and in order to get the toothpaste to come through the dispenser, we had to push a big white button, which wasn't difficult for Heinz and me, but was very difficult for the children. Plus, the opening for the toothpaste on the bottom of the dispenser was not even as wide as the opening on the toothpaste tube, so only a very small amount of toothpaste came out. When he installed it, Carol and Robert were too short to even reach the big white button on the wall, so they had to lean their entire bodies over the sink until their feet were off the floor, and with their stomachs on the edge of the sink, they often worked up a sweat, just trying to reach the button and muster the strength to push it hard enough. Often the kids just gave up. Needless to say, our toothpaste tube lasted for months and months.

At about the same time, Heinz announced another edict. He asked the kids to sit on the floor of the living room, while he sat in his favorite chair. The kids looked like "subjects" sitting at the feet of a king who was sitting on his throne. Then Heinz declared that no-one was allowed to use more than two sheets of toilet paper at a time. There were no excuses and no exceptions. I sat there and thought about how silly it was. The kids did not react at all. The simply nodded their heads and left the room when he was done speaking.

*****

That same year when Janet was 12, Carol 10, and Robert 9, Heinz was really putting pressure on the kids about behaving. "There will be no presents on Christmas if you misbehave," said Heinz to the children as we sat for dinner one evening. The kids did not even answer him. I felt like the life was being sucked out of me. Then on the Christmas Eve, they were "invited" to come down the stairs into the living room to see what presents were under the tree. Before they had even sat down, Heinz barked, "Janet, did you dry your hair?" Janet meekly and fearfully replied, "I thought I did," and ran back upstairs to dry her hair again. Then Heinz roared at Carol: "Where are your socks and slippers? You'll get sick if you come down with bare feet!" She also sought to appease him by saying "OK daddy, I'll do it," and running back upstairs. Nothing was said to Robert, but he followed his sisters upstairs anyway so Heinz wouldn't be able to find any fault with him.

A few minutes later after Janet re-dried her already dry hair; the three kids came back downstairs. They were a lot less excited than the first time, but they were still excited to see the gifts under the tree. Janet got some sweaters and Nancy Drew mystery books, Carol got a blue bike with a blue banana seat, and Robert got more G I Joe tanks and weapons. I was happy that they were pleased with the gifts I had picked out for them and that Heinz and I had wrapped together. But Heinz insisted on putting a "*rute*"—which is the German word for a stick used to hit a child on top of the packages. This was their father's reminder that the children had to behave, or there would be consequences. This *rute* looked more like a tree branch: it was brown, long, thin, and irregularly shaped. Heinz kept the *rute* and other sticks on top of the refrigerator, the edge always hung over so he could remind the children about it anytime. I began to notice the despair in my children. No matter how hard they tried, they were not going to please Heinz.

*****

Heinz and I often played pinochle with some of our German friends, Paula and Horst, Günter and Elfriede, and John and Theresa, and we usually socialized with them at our house. On one occasion, however, we were at Günter and Elfriede's home with the kids, who were 13, 11, and 10 at the time. While we played pinochle, our kids and Paula's son Jeffrey watched TV in a small room set up like an office, with a small sofa that could fit only three people, so one of the kids sat on the floor. Elfriede had brought the kids a small bowl of pretzels, too.

After about two and a half hours, the kids were bored: there was nothing else that they wanted to watch on television. Robert then sheepishly walked toward the kitchen and asked for more pretzels. "Of course, you can have more!" said Tante Elfriede, adding, "do you kids need any more soda or anything else?" Robert said no, and he thanked Tante Elfriede for the pretzels and took them back to the other kids and they devoured them within minutes.

I didn't think anything about this incident, because Robert had asked politely, he had thanked Elfriede, and he had shared with his sisters and Jeffrey. But in the car on the way home, Heinz did nothing but scream about the kids' poor manners: "I cannot *believe* you kids had the nerve to ask for more pretzels!" he yelled over and over again during the twenty-minute ride home. I was shocked, but I didn't say a word. I didn't argue with him. I didn't know what to do: Heinz was so angry, and I didn't know why.

I suspected that Heinz was suffering from depression—that's why he withdrew from the children (and from me), that's why he was unable to express any positive emotions, including love for me or his children, and that's why he fell asleep on the couch every night (even when friends visited us or we visited them). But he refused to discuss the subject with me. So as much as possible, Janet, Carol,

Robert, and I just tried not to anger Heinz or upset him in any way, but that was not easy to do.

By the time the kids were in high school, tension in our home was no longer creeping in; it was flowing like a river. When their report cards came home, Janet's was always a perfect set of "A's." Heinz looked at Janet's report card and nodded in silence. Carol was also very smart, and she got good grades, too, but one time, she got one "B" in science. I knew she hated that class: she had told me she was lucky to have gotten the "B" at all, since she and her lab partner had accidently started a fire during one of the lab experiments. No-one was hurt, and Carol's telling of the story was funny; even the science teacher had salvaged the potential disaster by teaching the kids what had happened to cause the fire. But when Heinz saw that Carol hadn't gotten straight "A's," he stabbed his finger into the card and demanded an explanation: "What happened here?"

Carol just sat very still; she didn't even answer Heinz. Robert had seen this happen before, and he had learned not to show his report card to Heinz; for some reason, Heinz never asked to see it. I hoped the storm would pass; sure enough, Heinz went to bed soon after his outburst. I knew my kids were smart and hardworking, but I couldn't defend them to Heinz; he would only have gotten angrier. I tried to console them by giving them all butterscotch candy for their good report cards, while reminding them "don't tell Daddy, he doesn't need to know." As if a little sugar could make things all better; if only it could have.

I believe Heinz loved his children; he just didn't know how to show that love. He continued to tease them as they got older, like the time he drove us all into the McDonald's parking lot and then just drove right out again (which gave "drive-through" a completely different meaning, that's for sure). I remember one time when Carol wanted to go over her friend Lydia's house: she and Lydia had been very good friends since they met in fifth grade; by ninth grade, either Lydia came over to our house after school, or Carol went to Lydia's.

The girls were very different: Lydia was much taller and thinner than my Carol, and she had long blonde hair and glasses. Lydia looked very bookish, very serious. In contrast, Carol was only 5' tall and an average weight, not thin like Lydia, but not heavy either (not like me!). Carol and Lydia also had very different interests: Lydia was very interested in science, animals, and zoology and Carol told me she had a rock collection in one of her dresser drawers. Carol, on the other hand, was terrible at science, and she really only liked to play outside sports. But the two girls genuinely liked each other, and they got along very well, so I was happy they spent so much time together.

One Saturday afternoon when they were in the ninth grade, Lydia invited Carol to come over so they could work on a history project that they were teaming up on. Carol could walk to Lydia's house if she crossed the fields behind our home and then trespassed through the neighbors' yards. Even if she walked the long way, on the main roads, it only took about ten minutes for Carol to get to Lydia's house. Normally, the walk was fun, but on that particular day, it was raining really hard, so Carol asked Heinz if he would drive her over to Lydia's house. I was no longer driving, after my panic attacks, so Carol knew only her father could take her.

But Heinz said, in a teasing tone, "Ach Carol, you can walk, a little rain never hurt anyone." I saw Carol stiffen, stung by this comment. And I felt my own face grow hot: I knew Lydia's mother, Margaret, had come by many times when it was raining to pick up Carol and Janet and drive them to school with her own kids. But I knew neither Carol nor I could argue with Heinz; he would have gotten angry and might have forbid Carol from going to visit at all. So I said nothing.

But Carol was getting older, and she was beginning to assert herself. I was stunned when she retorted, "Never mind, I'll just walk." Then she stormed out of the house, slamming the door behind her, and I saw her start to run down the street. It was raining buckets by this time, and when Heinz realized Carol would be soaked by the time she got to Lydia's, he got in the car and followed her. I saw Heinz pulled up alongside her and opened the passenger door without even coming to a complete stop, but she didn't even want to get in. She told him, "No thanks, dad, I am fine walking. I am OK. You don't need to drive me." She was already drenched anyway, but I knew she was also very hurt.

Carol's refusal to get in angered Heinz even more than her storming out of the house. He bellowed at her, "You had better get in the car, or you won't be going to Lydia's house today or for a long time ever again." He slammed on the brakes, and the car came to a complete stop. I'm sure Carol was frightened as she got in. She told me they didn't say another word to each other, and Heinz dropped her off at Lydia's house. Her jeans were soaked through, and even her socks and shoes were heavy from the water. Lydia's mother, Margaret, was surprised to see the state she was in, but Carol said she didn't ask Carol what had happened. Neither did Lydia. Margaret simply offered some of Lydia's clothes to wear, and she dried my daughter's clothes in her dryer. When Carol came home a few hours later, no-one said anything about the storm that had taken place both outside and within our family.

I realized that as I had tried to control my destiny by marrying someone so different from my own father, my children were beginning to form their own strategies for how they wanted to live their lives. I thought I could have the security that was lacking in my parent's marriage by marrying Heinz, who seemed to be so loyal, stable, and responsible. But our children were afraid of their father. I knew they felt they could never do anything to please him. I was worried about the children. Janet, I hoped would realize that Heinz was depressed, but I saw that she was becoming more introverted. Carol was becoming very angry and self-reliant. Robert was so insecure. And I was becoming more desperate and unsure what to do.

*****

"Taste and see that the Lord is good; blessed is the man who takes refuge in him." Psalm 34:8

—11—

Returning to Germany after 20 Years

"Going Home"

To go home can mean a lot of things. You arrive at your sister's home and she's so happy to see you. Right away, she offers you her favorite chair. "Put your feet up," she says.—you're home.

Your brother's in the kitchen making fresh-squeezed lemonade, just because you like it that way.—You're home.

Friends you didn't see for many years have tears of joy in their eyes to meet you again. A little bird busily trying to make a nest captures your attention. You haven't seen this type of bird for many years. Your heart rejoices.—You're home.

If you walk through your former hometown, the aroma of fresh-baked bread and sweet-smelling bakery goods automatically points your feet in their direction.—You're home.

The swaying branches of the chestnut trees seem to know you came for a visit and the sounds of a horse's footsteps have a familiar rhythm you loved so much when you were smaller.—You're home.

You listen to a wonderful concert. The music carries you away to your favorite place, a small room where you used to play with your dolls. You truly came home.

—Anita Plutte

In 1975, in the fall of Janet's senior year of high school, Heinz and I finally decided to go back to Germany. "Anita, I think we should go over there to see the parents, they are getting older, we may never see them again. Let's make the trip," he said, much to my surprise. We had saved enough money, and it had been more than 20 years since either of us had seen any family, except for those three weeks when my Mama was here. We left our three children home alone, with our friends Paula, Elfriede, and Lydia's mother, Margaret, to keep an eye on them.

Our first stop on the trip was East Germany. Now armed with a U.S. passport, the East German officials could not do anything to me for escaping illegally 20 years earlier. We took the train from West Germany into East Germany, where we had arranged to meet Renate in Chemnitz (which had been re-named Karl-Marx Stadt). Over the years, I had sent pictures to all the family, especially in Christmas cards, and Renate's family had done the same, although they could only process black-and-white pictures. I had recent pictures of all the family.

When the train drew closer to the station, I grew more and more excited. As the train slowed, I caught a glimpse of Renate waving a handkerchief to get my attention. My heart just stopped. Even Heinz had moist eyes. He too was emotional about the reunion. When the train wheeled screeched to a halt, I was already out of my seat and walking towards the door. My throat was a big lump; I couldn't talk. Tears flowed from my eyes down to my chin. I didn't wipe my face, I just kept moving towards Renate. Renate's husband, Roland, was there too. I had only met him a few times before. When I was free of the people on either side of me, Renate and I saw no one except each other.

For about 10 minutes, we just hugged and cried and smiled. We still looked so much alike, except that Renate was blonde and still much slimmer. Otherwise, our facial features—round cheeks, high cheekbones, smiling eyes—were identical. We definitely looked like sisters. Heinz followed me, and he too cried when he embraced Renate and shook Roland's hand.

And then the 20 years just melted away. We talked to each other as though it had only been a week. For those 20 years, we could only write letters. And my German often failed me. I was actually much better in English at this point. I included the words, "ok, right, you know," and probably a few others in my sentences all the time. My sister Renate thought it was funny. She NEVER asked me to repeat the entire sentence in German. By the end of the trip, everyone was saying "OK."

Roland had a very small white car, one of the few people in East Germany who had gotten one. At that time, there was about a 10-year waiting list. Most of the cars were small and looked alike. We four got in Roland's car and drove to my Mama's apartment. It was there that I met my 18-year-old niece, Renate's daughter Marion for the first time. Marion was a very sweet young lady who was really close to her mother, Renate. My Mama had prepared a lunch of rolls, lunch meat, butter, and coffee and cake. We sat down and talked about everything that happened to us in the last 20 years. I got caught up on all the family, taking it all in and yet feeling like I was dreaming at the same time. Heinz felt the same way and without communicating it, we knew we had done the right thing by coming. Heinz was anxious to see his family, especially his father, too.

We spent the next few days with my Mama, and on the weekend, all of my siblings and extended family arrived. The next day, we visited Heinz's parents. I could tell Heinz was excited when we walked over to Paul's house the next morning. Heinz walked so fast, his face was red; his thoughts must have been racing. When Paul answered the door, both men were overcome with emotion, and they cried as they embraced. Marta invited them in, and the two men began to talk. How was it even possible to get through 25 years of lost time? Paul had so many questions for Heinz. He wanted to know how he liked living in America. Paul's brother Fritz had died, but he asked about his brother Wilhelm. I was amazed as I watched the two men. Paul was taller, maybe 5' 10", while Heinz was only 5' 4" tall. Their body motions were identical. They walked the same way, and their facial features were identical. They both pounded their fists on the table when they were excited. I thought to myself, *this is exactly what Heinz will look like when he grows old.*

Heinz proudly showed his father pictures of his home and our three children. Heinz beamed when he saw Paul's nodding approval as he looked at all the pictures. From an East German perspective, an average American looked wealthy. We did not say anything, but I could tell it bothered Heinz that his father still did not have indoor plumbing. The afternoon flew by, and Heinz and I were next going to visit my Mama to stay with her for a few days. Heinz and I had brought presents for each of the families. Blue jeans were a big hit, and so was the chocolate and coffee.

That evening we went back to my Mama's apartment where a handsome brown-haired 25-year-old man greeted me at the door. It was my brother, Karl-Heinz! He really had no memory of me because he was only five when I left, and now he was there in front of me, a grown and confident young man. It only took one minute for and Karl-Heinz and me to unconsciously acknowledge that we were family and loved each other.

But it was a little painful for me to see my mother in the apartment without my father. "When will Papa be over?" I asked, probably sounding more like a child looking for her daddy than a grown woman of 43.

"Ach, Anita, Papa is on his way," said my Mama. I was glad for this and stayed in the enjoyable moments of getting to know my brother as a man. "Die Janet looks just like my Marion," said Renate when I showed her some of the pictures, "and your Robert really looks like Karli, too," she continued. As we talked more, I realized that hardly anyone even owned a home in East Germany. Everyone lived in apartments. I tried to explain how different things are in America. American kids are different. They are freer in how they act. They have so much. I could never imagine living in East Germany again, not after experiencing the freedoms in America, although I did not say that to my sister.

"So Anita, I really want to know how you and Heinz are doing. I always told you he was a good man," my Mama said when she and I were alone.

"Oh, Mama, he really is a good provider. But I think everything that happened to him as a child somehow prevents him from being totally happy. He always needs to find something to complain about. Last Christmas, the kids were so excited about their gifts. They all got new board games and clothes. It was almost like he couldn't stand the fact that they were happy, and so he threatened that the gifts would be returned if they acted out. Of course, the kids never act out, they are a little afraid of Heinz anyway. I was never afraid of Papa. It is so different for me."

"Ach Anita," said my Mama, "just do the best you can. Heinz is a good person." My Mama just shrugged it off, though I would have liked to talk more. But it was time for dinner.

She served roladen, rot kraut, and brot for dinner. This was an expensive and luxurious dinner for East Germans. "Oh, Mama, I can't believe we are home. This is a dream. And Karl-Heinz, how can this be possible?" It was wonderful to be at a large table with my Mama, Renate, Roland, Karl-Heinz, and his wife Christine.

A few days later, my Papa rented a big wagon, like a wagon used for a hay ride, large enough for all of my siblings to be together. My Mama came along, too. We went to the surrounding areas of the little town of Frohburg, to a pottery factory and a big lake nearby. We ate at the Lindervorwerke Restaurant in Kohren/Sahlis. My Papa paid for everything. On another day, we went shopping in Chemnitz with my Papa. The Volkskunst-Geschaeft store sold all the wood carvings hand crafted in the Ezrgebirge region (the mountains in the surrounding areas). There I saw a pyramide that I really liked. It had a manger scene along the bottom, angels along the top near the wings that spin, and glass bells. It was made of natural wood, and all hand-carved. My Papa saw that I was looking at it. "Do you like it?" he asked me. I did not want him to buy it for me, but he could tell that I really liked it. Heinz said, "Ach Anita, you already have that large white pyramide that your Papa bought you before. You do not need another pyramide." We bought some gifts to take back to our friends in Philadelphia. Then Heinz and I walked out of the store.

As we walked out, I saw my Papa was already waiting for us outside the store. He had a huge smile on his face, and a triumphant look about him. "Here, Anita, that is for you," he said as he handed me a large box wrapped in brown paper. I knew immediately that my Papa had bought that pyramide for me. Heinz just looked away and did not say anything.

Then Renate and I spent a day with my Papa, while Heinz visited with his family. This was one my favorite days of the entire trip. We visited Chemnitz (which was called Karl-Marx Stadt then) and walked all around the city. My old school (my *Grundschule*) had been rebuilt in the same location. But Ludwig Strasse was not rebuilt, and I was really disturbed by this. All the debris had been cleared away, but the buildings were not replaced. Later that evening, my Papa, Renate, and I went to the Opera House in Chemnitz, the same opera house that my Papa had played at. We saw *Die Lustigen Weiber von Windsor*, which means *The Happy Women from Windsor.* The Opera House was different from how I remembered it. It looked like a white bed sheet was used as the curtain between acts. I felt bad because this image confirmed the lack of progress in East Germany. However, the performance was exceptional.

Heinz had also spent a wonderful day with his father. They walked around Frohburg and just talked. Heinz also enjoyed seeing Christa and her family, and he especially enjoyed meeting his brother Winfried's family. Winfried had grown to be a very tall man, over six feet tall, so Heinz did not look so much like the older brother anymore, but Heinz was still paternal in his actions and feelings towards Winfried. Heinz asked Winfried if he liked the wetsuit Heinz bought and shipped to him from America. Wetsuits were not available in East Germany, and Heinz was very happy that he could provide this for his younger brother.

Before we left East Germany, we left most of our clothes there for our family. Even though our clothes were modest by American standards, they were luxury items to the East Germans. There just wasn't anything for them to buy.

Next, we went to West Germany and traced the path Heinz took as he fled from East Germany. We stayed with his friends who had helped him as he first fled. We saw the man who had employed Heinz in Osterfeld, as he saved money to come to America. Finally, we stayed with two of Heinz's cousins who lived in Bavaria. They were two sisters, both in their late forties, who had never been married. As the two cousins were driving us to the airport, I remarked, "Well Heinz, we traced a complete circle of your entire life. After reconnecting with your family, we saw everyone you had been with or worked with up until the time you came to America. How wonderful." "Ach, Anita, this was a fantastic trip. It was right to visit our parents. They are getting old, and we may never see them again." Heinz was so relaxed on that trip. It was the happiest Heinz had been in a long time.

When we came home, I was so proud of my three children. The house was in perfect shape. Janet and Carol had baked us a pound cake and written "Welcome Home" in chocolate frosting. Lydia's mother, Margaret, had made a "Welcome Home" poster for our front door. I had missed the children so much, and I was glad to see them again.

Yet after a few days, it was like we had never been away. "Robert, where are my shoes? I told you to never move my shoes from the front door," Heinz said when he was ready to go to work.

"You moved them, Daddy, you put them in the basement to dry because it was raining," said Robert.

Heinz said nothing and walked to get them. I put the food on the table. Everyone ate. Little was said. After dinner, the kids did their homework and went to their bedrooms. All our feelings of excitement from the Germany trip had disappeared.

Heinz said he had wanted to go back to Germany because his parents and my parents were getting older, and he thought we should see them again. Any time earlier, when I mentioned a possible trip to Germany, he typically said it was out of the question because there was no money for that. Oddly enough, though, there really wasn't any change in our financial situation; somehow, Heinz just felt a strong need to go back.

*****

"Your love, O Lord, reaches to the heavens, your faithfulness to the skies." Psalm 36:5

—12—

Janet Could Not Wait to Leave Home

By the time she was in her mid-teens, Janet was a quiet, scholarly, insecure, and shy young woman. She guarded everything she said, with everyone, and thus risked speaking very rarely. She was also self-conscious about being overweight: even though she was well-liked by her teachers, our neighbors, and her many friends, she told me she felt like "a bottomless pit that could never get filled up." No matter how many positive messages were given to her—by me or anyone else—she never felt good enough, and she just kept trying harder and harder to be the very best person she could possibly be.

I was very close to Janet...in some ways, I felt more like a friend than her mother, and I think she realized that even when she was very young. She was my oldest, of course, and looked so much like my sister Erika, and she was very mature. We freely talked about everything, and Janet told me she felt she could tell me anything and I would love her no matter what. Of course, that was true! I loved all my children: they filled me with so much happiness, and they were the best part of my marriage to Heinz.

But Janet didn't feel that way about her father. She wanted him to love her and be proud of her, but she told me she always felt she was never quite good enough, and she was always afraid she would make him angry. Heinz *was* frightening when he got angry: he had a very loud, booming voice when he yelled that sent chills down my spine, and he frequently flew into a rage over what seemed like very small things to me and the children. We never quite seemed to be able to predict 100% what would set him off, so we lived very carefully not to disturb him in any way and to do everything he wanted. I don't know what had happened to the shy boy I had met at dance class, the boy who had been so protective of his younger brother but was now so harsh and demanding of his children.

*****

Janet had always wanted to learn how to play a musical instrument. When she was in elementary school, free organ classes were offered for 10 weeks, and she loved playing the organ. My Papa had been a musician, so I was thrilled that she was interested in music. But organs were so expensive, and when she asked Heinz and me if we could get an organ so she could learn to play it, I knew what Heinz would say—that we just didn't have enough money for such frivolity. So Janet started an "organ fund" that she and Carol and Robert all contributed to, out of their allowance. By the time Janet was in her senior year of high school, we still hadn't bought an organ, and there was only $137 in the organ fund. Janet realized there was no way her dream would come true. For her 16th birthday, Janet's high-school friends all pitched in and bought her a guitar. One of our neighbors offered guitar lessons, and Janet insisted on paying for them herself, with money she had earned by working part time in a restaurant and from teaching German classes at a local church on Saturdays. Heinz told her he hated guitar music and that he didn't want to hear her playing. But Janet was undeterred: she practiced in her room, with the door shut, strumming as softly as she possibly could. Her teacher told her that she needed to strum more vigorously, but I knew she would never really have the chance to practice playing that way. Still, she was doing what she wanted, finally learning to play an instrument.

She was also spending less and less time at home. One day, she came home from school and realized she had left her guitar at school. She told me, "Mom, I am going to drive back there to get it, and then my friends and I will be going to dinner at a pizza place. I really don't know when I will be home." I let her go; because I knew she was trying to stay away from Heinz as much as possible. She had gotten involved in student government with some friends, and she never came directly home from school anymore. When she did come home, she ate dinner and went upstairs to do her homework. It was obvious to all of us that she was simply trying to avoid her father.

Two days later, Heinz came home from work and confronted Janet at dinner. “I heard you left your guitar at school. How can someone so smart be so stupid at the same time?” he asked her. Janet rushed to explain: “It was an accident, Daddy. Anyway, I got the guitar back the same day. It’s not like it was stolen.” That was already far too many words for Heinz, and he yelled at Janet across the table: “Don’t talk back to me! You should appreciate the fact that you have a guitar and take care of it. You don’t realize how good you kids have it here!” Janet recoiled into her chair and didn’t say another word. No-one did.

There were situations, though, when Janet did not acquiesce to her father’s wishes, if she felt something he asked her to do was really wrong. One day in the spring of her junior year, she came home from high school and noticed that our dog Prinz was lying down in the grass, listless, and he was foaming at the mouth. Prinz was a mutt, mostly beagle but part German shepherd. He was brown with dark markings, actually a very cute little dog, and we all really loved him. When Janet noticed Prinz was ill and mentioned it to us, Heinz said, “We don’t have any money for vet bills. Who knows what he got into? He could have eaten a dead animal and gotten rabies. Let’s just take him to the vet to have him put down.”

Janet was shocked: she couldn’t believe what Heinz was saying. Prinz had been our dog for eight years—he was *family*. It was true that Prinz often ran free behind our fenced-in yard, where there were woods and fields, and sometimes he would be gone for hours.

But maybe he *didn't* have rabies! Yet Heinz wanted to end his life without even finding out what was wrong.

I didn't say anything. No one did. But Janet refused to take Prinz to the vet to be euthanized. I could see that Heinz was angry that Janet wouldn't do what he said, but he couldn't force her to get in the car, and I doubted he would take Prinz to the vet. He started to walk away from Janet, shaking his head in disgust, then he turned around and retorted, "OK, Janet, if you think you can save Prinz, take a look in these medical books and see if you can figure out what is wrong with him. Read what it says," he commanded. We had a few medical reference books, which Janet pulled off the shelf, and she spent about an hour reading through them. Finally, she turned to look at her father. Her hands were on her hips, her voice was uneven as she said to her father, "I don't know what is wrong with Prinz, and I don't care if you yell at me or not. I just don't think he should be killed. Let's just give him a few days and see if he gets better."

And Heinz backed down. "Ok, but you clean up whatever mess he makes." A few days later, Prinz was back to his old self and the issue was never brought up again.

*****

Janet was only 16 when she was in her senior year of high school, but it was clear she was ready to build her own life and go off to college. She wasn't sure what she wanted to do career-wise, but she knew she wanted to go to college, and she believed she would find a career path along the way. She also wanted to go to a college that was far enough away so she could live there, but close enough so she could easily come home to visit. So she applied only to colleges in Pennsylvania and New Jersey. I was happy that she would be close by, but I also began to realize it was unlikely that Janet would ever live with us again; because of how strained her relationship was with her father.

At the same time, I was also starting to get restless: I wanted to find a better job than working at the German club or the luncheonette. I even thought about possibly going to college myself. After all, with Janet getting ready for college and Carol and Robert both in high school, I didn't really need to be home all day, and our family needed more money coming in so that we would be able to pay for their college educations. I broached the subject with Heinz as carefully as I could: I spoke softly and begged him to allow me to look for work.

"Ach Anita, why would you want to do that? You just stay home and cook and clean. I'll take care of the money," he said. I was so disappointed, but I did not argue with him. Later that evening, as I sat in the kitchen with Janet, I remember saying, "It's OK, Janet. Your father is a good provider, and I really like cooking. It's just that I would love to go to college and do something in medicine." I had always enjoyed science, ever since my first job back in East Germany when I worked for a company that made chemicals. I had been good at science in school, too, and if I had been able to go to college, I would have liked to become a doctor myself. But that wasn't possible for me, given my family's situation in East Germany, and I was fortunate to even come to the United States so I could create a better life for my children.

Janet was also interested in medicine and science in general, so Heinz made it clear to her that he wanted her to become a doctor. She confided in me that, deep down inside, she was afraid to be a doctor. She worried that she would made a mistake and that someone might die or be injured because of something she did, and she told me she would never be able to live with that and was really afraid to go down that path.

To appease her father, Janet told him she did not want to be in school for eight years before she could start earning money, but if she could get into an accelerated BA/MD program, where she would be able to earn both a bachelor's and medical degrees in only 5 or 6 years, she would do that. She thought this was a safe strategy because those programs were extremely competitive, and she thought she would never be accepted. To her surprise, however, she was accepted into both of the programs she applied for, so now she had to decide what to do.

We discussed it, and she told me she just knew this was not the right path for her; she knew she could handle the class work, but she was so afraid of the patient care aspect of medicine. Heinz was adamant that he wanted Janet to accept one of these positions, but she decided not to. Her father was furious with her. He distanced himself even farther from her, and he told me if she did not go to medical school, he would not pay for her college. He said, "If you are not going to be a doctor, why would you bother to even go to college? Girls should just stay home and take care of the household."

I didn't know what to do: there was no way to argue with Heinz, and it was unlikely he would change his mind, so Janet and I hoped she would be able to get a scholarship. She said she felt this was the only way she would be able to go to college—if she somehow won a full scholarship. Fortunately, she had ranked first in her high school class for the past two years, so we thought she might have a chance at the full scholarships to Philadelphia colleges that were available to students who graduated first in their class from a Philadelphia high school. I felt bad that she was under so much pressure for the rest of her senior year in high school, as she studied even harder. She told me if she didn't get a full scholarship, she hoped she would at least get enough financial aid that she could work her way through college for the rest of the money she would need for tuition and expenses.

Meanwhile, Heinz seemed to resent her new independence: Janet was spending less time at home and more time either studying at the local library or with friends. I was happy she had friends who made her feel good about herself; because I knew she felt her father was constantly at odds with her, about everything, including her appearance. Janet was overweight, and she had been all her life—as I was.

Even when I lived in East Germany and we didn't have enough to eat, I was chubby. At the age of 16, however, she was more than ever aware of it: she had never had a boyfriend, and I knew she was self-conscious about how her clothes fit her.

I tried to reassure Janet that her weight didn't matter as long as she was healthy, but Heinz had the opposite opinion. Each morning, before Janet left for school, he insisted that she do calisthenics in front of him, at 5 am while he ate breakfast. Even though I protested, Heinz didn't listen to me, so Janet just endured it as patiently as she could. It was clear, though, that she couldn't wait to get out of the house for school. At least school was a safe environment.

*****

Janet's relationship with her father got even worse towards the end of her senior year, when she had a minor car accident. Because I didn't drive anymore since my panic attacks, Janet often dropped me off and picked me up if I needed to go somewhere. One night, I attended a parent-teacher conference for Robert at his middle school, and Janet came to pick me up around 9:00pm. It was dark, and she was tired, but Heinz had been even more tired from a long day at work, so Janet had come for me. When she pulled up for me in the parking lot of the school, I saw that both doors on the passenger side were dented, and I asked her, "Janet, what happened to the car?"

She told me she didn't know, but when she came to look at the damage, she remembered that as she had turned right out of our development onto the main road, she had heard something, but she didn't know what it was, so she had just kept going. She now realized what must have happened as she made the turn: there was a telephone pole there, and she must have cut the corner too close and hit the pole. I didn't care about the damage to the car, and I was relieved that she was OK, though I was concerned that she hadn't realized what happened at the time. I realized she hadn't been driving for very long—she had only gotten her license a few months earlier—and I certainly knew how difficult it was to drive at night.

Janet was terrified at the prospect of telling her father what happened. Fortunately, he was asleep when we came home. I told her I would talk to Heinz in the morning. As soon as I had served him his breakfast and he had eaten something, I sat down and said as gently as I could, "Heinz, Janet hit a telephone pole last night when she turned right out of our street. She didn't realize it. The car has some damage, and she's upset enough about what happened. Please don't make her feel any worse than she already does. The car doesn't need to be fixed right away; it's running fine, and when we can save up to have it repaired."

Heinz immediately went outside to look at the car. I went with him, hoping I could explain further what had happened. When I looked back at the house, I saw Janet watching us from her bedroom window. Heinz was shaking his head in disgust and confusion.

When he went back inside, he ran up the stairs and into her room, already firing questions at her: "How did this happen? Did you black out? Does your head hurt? Should we take you to the doctor?" She told him she was OK and that she hadn't blacked out, that she was just really tired when she left to pick me up. At this, he shook his head again and said, "I just don't know how someone so smart can be so stupid," a statement he made all too often to all of our children. When I objected, he just repeated it, and Janet and I knew the best thing to do at that point was to keep quiet and let him cool down. Janet didn't even answer him any more when he asked her over and over again how this could have happened.

*****

A few days later, Janet found out she would be graduating #1 in her class of more than 1,000 students, and because of that, she had been offered a fully paid scholarship to the University of Pennsylvania. She had also gotten a near-perfect score on her SATs. I was so proud of her, and I hoped Heinz was too. But I could also see her pulling away from us. She seemed increasingly sad and distant, and I knew she was withdrawing as a way of coping. But Janet's distance from our family caused me physical pain. I didn't know what to do. I was sure Janet knew that I loved her, and I hoped that was enough.

*****

On graduation night, I was so proud of Janet. I had a daughter who was going to graduate first in her class of more than 1,000 students and win many of the academic awards and also a full scholarship to college for all 4 years. George Washington High School's Class of 1976 and my Janet was Number One!

But Heinz was still angry with Janet because she had decided to decline two offers for 5- or 6-year doctorate programs, one at Lehigh University and the other at Penn State/Jefferson. Janet had made her decision to study biochemistry and the University of Pennsylvania, and Heinz wanted her to be a doctor. On her graduation night, Heinz decided to pick a fight about it. "So Janet, what are you really going to do with your degree from the University of Pennsylvania? You could be a doctor! I don't understand why you don't want to do that. Until you have a profession that you can earn money with, there's nothing to celebrate. I don't even want to go to your graduation," Heinz screamed.

By this point in her life, Janet was so numb to her father. "Whatever you want to do is up to you," she said quietly, "I have to leave early for the ceremony, so I am leaving right now. It doesn't matter to me if you come or not." She carried her white graduation cap and gown in her arm and she left. I felt like I was going to faint. "Heinz, that is our daughter, and I am so proud of her. I am going even if I have to walk." It was the first time I had ever raised my voice back to Heinz.

Yet I knew that if we walked to the graduation, we would be late—it was almost two miles away—and I didn't want to miss it. So I thought of asking Mrs. Cella, one of our neighbors, to drive me and Carol and Robert. As I started to call her, though, I just lost control. I couldn't stop sobbing, so I hung up the phone.

Without saying another word, Carol stormed out the door and headed towards Mrs. Cella's house to ask her for a ride. How embarrassing it would be to explain that we want to go Janet's graduation—who, by the way, is graduating first in the class and getting most of the awards—and Heinz doesn't want to go! Once Heinz realized how angry we all were, he relented.

"OK Anita, let's go to the graduation," he said. Our dining room table had already been set up for a buffet. I had invited Janet's friends and Paula and Horst, Elfriede and Günter who were also our good friends, and some of the neighbors, including the Cellas to celebrate after the ceremony. So Heinz, Carol, and Robert, and I got into the car. No one said a word. My head was throbbing and my heart was aching. Heinz couldn't even let me enjoy that very special day. He had ruined it.

But when we arrived, Heinz saw a vendor selling small bouquets of red carnations for people to purchase for their special graduates. As we approached the gate to the football field, Heinz bought a bouquet of the flowers for Janet and asked me to hold onto them until the ceremony was over. I felt a little bit better: at least he was trying to make amends. No one clapped louder and cheered more than I did that night as Janet's name was called out over and over again.

When Janet stepped off the stage, I handed the flowers Heinz had bought back to him to give to her, but he shook his head and asked me to give them to her. I think he didn't want to do anything more to spoil her celebration. When we got home and people started coming to our house for the party we had planned for her, Heinz went upstairs and went to bed early, as he often did, although this was even earlier than usual. Janet had a great time with her friends and our neighbors and family, and the party lasted until midnight, while Heinz stayed upstairs, asleep.

*****

During the summer after high school, Janet worked as a tour guide for the Philadelphia Bicentennial celebration in 1976. She commuted by train into downtown Philadelphia every day. One day, Janet had missed the early train coming home, and when she came in the door, Heinz started shouting at her. "Janet, what have you been doing all this time? I saw you at the train station coming off the early train."

"No, dad, I missed the early train by two minutes, so I had to wait for the next train. You must have seen someone else at the train station," she said calmly.

"Don't lie to me, I KNOW it was YOU!" Heinz's volume had increased.

"No, daddy, it must have been someone else," Janet replied again meekly.

"I want to know what you were doing all this time. Where have you been? Who have you been with?" he insisted.

At this, Janet lost her temper and shouted back, "You're right, I was smoking and doing drugs and getting myself pregnant. Oh, by the way, here is a gift I picked up at the museum for you today," and she tossed a small bag of coal at Heinz.

With that, Heinz flew into a rage, and I told Janet to run upstairs to her room and lock and barricade the door. I then tried to plead with him that he should believe Janet. She had NEVER done anything to cause us to mistrust her.

"Anita, I saw her. She was lying to us," he growled.

"No Heinz, you are WRONG," I screamed.

He then stormed out of his chair and decided to take a walk in the woods.

Janet went out with her friends that night and came home after Heinz was asleep. Janet and Heinz didn't speak to each other again for the rest of the summer. I couldn't believe how our family was disintegrating in front of my very eyes. All I could do was hope things would get better when Janet left for college and she and Heinz both had time and distance to put things in perspective.

*****

When it was time for Janet to move to college, Heinz agreed to make only one trip to take her there and help her move in, even though the campus was only an hour away. So Janet had packed all of her stuff into a foot locker and just one suitcase. Carol and Robert wanted to go with us to see her off, so that meant only having the trunk of the car and our laps for all her belongings. Carol, Robert, Janet, and I each held a bag or suitcase on our laps while Heinz drove. It was August, and it was still a very hot summer day, so we were very uncomfortable in the hot car. Heinz could have put on the air conditioning, but he didn't, and we all knew not to bother to ask for it. There was total silence in the car for the entire trip.

As we pulled up to the drop-off point, we were directed to unload our things, and park the car in a lot about 40 feet away.

"You just take your stuff out here, Janet," said Heinz. Janet, Carol, and Robert unloaded everything, and the four of us helped her carry her meager belongings to her dorm room on the third floor of the quad at the University of Pennsylvania. Heinz stayed with the car and never even said goodbye to her. I was upset at the way he was acting, but I didn't know what to say to him, and I didn't want to make a scene on the bustling campus.

When we got upstairs, we saw that Janet's room-mate had not yet arrived, so Carol, Robert, and I lingered a few minutes to hug her and wish her well. I told Janet how proud I was of her. I wanted to stay longer, but I knew Heinz wanted to get home.

As I turned around for a last wave goodbye, my heart broke to see my daughter sitting in an empty dorm room, not knowing anyone and beginning life on her own, carrying all the hurts of the last year that just would not heal. Maybe now she would find her happiness. I sobbed as I returned to the car. I wished I could have stayed longer and embraced her. I saw Janet's pain, and I shared it. I could not believe my husband was unable to see how wonderful Janet was, what a precious human being our daughter really was. It felt like a stab through my heart.

I did not say one word in the car on the way home. Neither did Carol and Robert. At that moment, I felt like I was married to a complete stranger. I was afraid to confront or engage Heinz when he was angry. I felt completely helpless. I never considered leaving. I simply did not know what to do. Heinz had often directed his hostility towards Janet. Nothing she did was ever good enough for him. And I felt helpless to protect her.

I have always tried to look for the good and positive in every situation, but on this particular day, I could find nothing good or positive. My normally colorful vibrant world lost all its splendor and color. Everything just looked black to me.

*****

"He who fears the Lord has a secure fortress, and for his children it will be a refuge." Proverbs 14:26

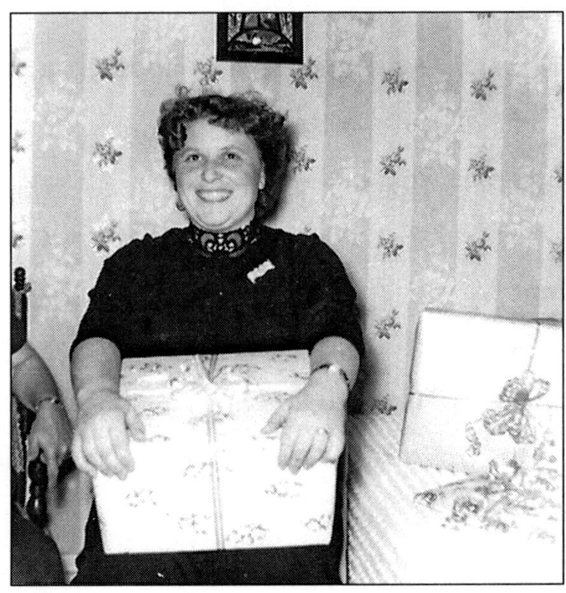

My bridal shower, in December 1956, only a few weeks after I had arrived in the United States. We didn't have this custom in Germany, so it was a surprise (and a bit of an embarrassment!) for me to receive such nice gifts from my new friends and family in Philadelphia.

Wedding day, January 19, 1957 only a month after I came to the U.S.: I didn't know the American custom of wearing a long, white gown but I really liked this copper-colored dress. This is in the Feltonville Lutheran Church in the Northeast section of Philadelphia.

Such happy times: Heinz and me with baby Janet, in our home at 9912 Medway Road in Northeast Philadelphia.

Janet approximately two years old on the rocking horse that Heinz made for her.

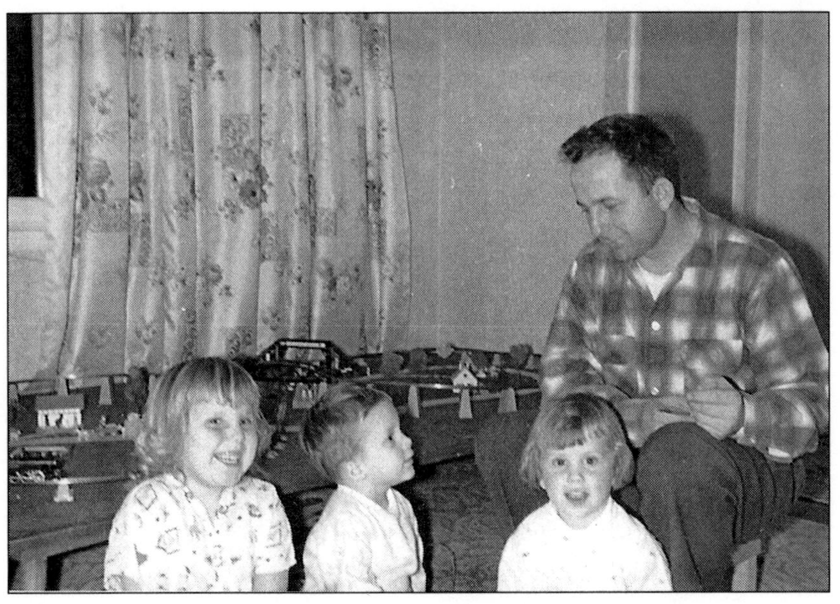

Janet, Robert, and Carol with Heinz in December 1964. Janet is five years old, Robert is two years old, and Carol is three years old. Heinz always set up the trains around Christmastime.

Easter Sunday 1972: We are standing in front of the garage of our home—me, Janet, age 13, Carol, age 10, and Robert, age 9.

Heinz and I visited East Germany in 1975 for the first time since we left two decades earlier: this is Erika, Hans, Mama, me, Karl-Heinz, and Renate. The last time I saw my sisters and brothers they were young adults and children—it was wonderful to see them again.

On the same trip to Germany in 1975, Renate, Papa, and I went to the opera.

PART III

A BROKEN FAMILY

—13—

The Horrible Accident

During her first semester, Janet came home only when it was absolutely necessary. We talked on the phone occasionally, but the first time we saw her was Thanksgiving. I missed her terribly, and I was so happy to see her. She told me university life was wonderful: she loved her classes, she was meeting so many new and different people, and she enjoyed her job in the dining service office. There was plenty to do on the weekends, and she even visited her friends from high school who went to college nearby, or they came to visit her. The Thanksgiving weekend flew by, and I was sorry to see her return to school, but I couldn't really be sad: she was so happy and seemed to much more at peace since she had started college. Plus, I knew she would be home for much longer over the Christmas break.

That Christmas, in 1976, was very unusual. Heinz was very generous with the gifts we gave the children that year. He had asked each of them what they really wanted, which he had never done before: I had always taken care of choosing and wrapping their presents. This year, Robert told his father he wanted a 10-speed bike, Carol said she would like a typewriter for school, and Janet had asked for a camera with a built-in flash. Then Heinz went out and bought everything by himself. He had never spent so much money on Christmas gifts before. I couldn't believe it! And on Christmas Eve, when we all gathered to celebrate, the children were all surprised by their gifts. It was a wonderful Christmas, and I hoped that something had changed in our family, for the better.

*****

A few weeks later, in mid-January 1977, Janet was getting ready to return for her second semester. It was the last Saturday of her winter break, and we were all home except for Heinz. Carol and Janet were reading in the living room, and Robert was doing homework in his bedroom. I was doing laundry, and Heinz was out, helping remodel the kitchen of a friend of our friends Paula and Horst. Heinz was a skilled carpenter, and he often helped friends with home-renovation projects: he enjoyed doing this work, and sometimes he even made a little extra money.

When he was late coming home, I started to worry because he was so punctual. There had been a heavy snow storm the previous day, though, and Heinz had gotten home about 2 hours late the night before. I knew that traffic was probably very slow because of the snow-covered roads, but I hoped it wasn't treacherous as well.

Then the phone rang. It was Paula, telling me that something had happened to Heinz. I don't really remember much about that call. There had been a fire at the house where Heinz was working, and all we knew was that he had burned his hands. About 20 minutes later, Paula and Horst came to pick me up and take me to the hospital. Janet, Carol and Robert were alarmed, but I didn't want them coming with me until I knew more about Heinz's injuries.

When I spoke to the emergency room doctors, they told me Heinz had 3rd-degree burns over 60% of his body. He was on oxygen, and they let me see him. He held up his hands as if to say, *Look at my hands, they are so badly burned, I will never be able to work again.* He couldn't speak, and neither could I. His hands were blackish, his fingers looked like big blisters stuck together, although they were somewhat bandaged already. He was sedated, the doctor explained, otherwise, he would be screaming in pain. I could see in his eyes the terror that he had experienced and was experiencing. There wasn't anything more that needed to be said. We both knew this was going to be a terrifying journey and our lives would never be the same.

The doctors wouldn't let me see the rest of his body. One of the doctors explained that he was burned so badly that his organs were exposed. In fact, if it had not been for the leather belt he was wearing his entire body would have been burned. As he said this, the doctor's voice was shaking. He was a young man, maybe in his early thirties.

He admitted he had never seen anything like this before, nothing this bad. That's when he told me they would be moving him to the burn center: he explained, "I'm sorry, Mrs. Plutte, but we are not equipped to take care of severe burn victims. We have already called for another ambulance, which will take him to the Burn Center." Then he put his hand on my shoulder and said gently, "I think you really need to pray." I couldn't even think of what questions I should ask. Heinz was completely covered by the white hospital sheets and only his head was visible. I had never seen my husband like this: he was always so strong, so powerful, and now he looked so terrible. My heart went out to him, but my brain was just numb.

*****

I didn't understand how this could have happened, but Heinz had been able to speak to Horst when they first got to the hospital, and then Horst had talked to his friend Joe, the owner of the house where Heinz had been working. Joe and his wife had gone to the store to buy sandwiches for lunch, and Heinz had continued working. He was using glue to resurface their kitchen cabinets when it ignited from the pilot light, and Heinz had been set on fire. He couldn't get out of the kitchen, because Joe had helped him move the refrigerator out of the way, and it was blocking the only exit from the kitchen to the rest of the house. There was a kitchen door to the outside, but it needed a key to unlock it, which Heinz didn't have and Joe and his wife weren't there. Heinz had been trapped in the kitchen.

Eventually, while he was engulfed in flames, he struggled until he could move the refrigerator enough to squeeze by, and then he ran through a glass door in the basement to get outside and roll in the snow. By then, a young man from down the street came running to the house with a fire extinguisher. Heinz went back into the house with the fire extinguisher to try to put out the fire: I'm sure he felt responsible for starting the fire, and he was going to do everything he could to put it out. By the time the fire trucks arrived, the fire was nearly extinguished. The firemen could not believe their eyes when they found Heinz standing in the middle of the kitchen with a fire extinguisher and the extent of burns on his body.

When Joe and his wife returned from the store, Heinz was being treated on a stretcher and getting ready to be taken to the hospital in an ambulance. Their house was severely fire damaged. Heinz just kept saying, "I'm so sorry, I'm so sorry about your house." Joe and his wife felt terrible—not about their house, but about Heinz's injuries, which they could tell were severe. "We were only gone for twenty minutes. We wanted to buy some good lunch meat to give him for lunch. He was working so hard and doing such a good job," Joe said.

*****

The next morning, Janet drove me to the Burn Center; we left Carol and Robert at home because we thought we should see Heinz first before the younger children did. I was a mess. I could not stop crying; I just felt so bad for Heinz and for what had happened to him and all that he was suffering.

When we got to the burn center, the nurses told us that before we could see him, we had to go through a special process to prevent infection to Heinz: we had to wash our hands up to our elbows with a special brown disinfectant soap, then put on a face mask, shoe covers, a hair net and a gown, and then we waited in a special waiting room since he was permitted only two people at a time, and a nurse was with him when we got there. When we were ushered into the area where he was being cared for, I went in first, alone, to talk to the doctors and the nurses. I wanted to protect the children from the bad news that the doctors were telling me – even Janet. I wanted the children to believe that he had a chance. Later Janet came in and joined me.

By the next day, Heinz looked much worse. If I had not known he was my husband, I would have never recognized him. His eyelashes and eyebrows were burned off. His face was swollen, like one big blister. His lips were puffy and completely white. Fluid seemed to fill his entire face, it was distorted. I could barely find his eyes in the fluidic blister. To talk to him, I had to put my ear right up to his mouth, and then I could hear what he was saying. His voice sounded like him, just very faint. I was glad he was conscious and recognized us and knew we were there for him. I spoke to him in German, telling him everything would be OK, even though I could see everything was *not* OK. We visited with him for a few minutes, and then the nurse asked us to leave so she could change his bandages.

The Burn Center was such a sad place, a terrible place—not in the quality of care, which is excellent, but because most patients are in horrible pain, and most do not survive. In every room, there were people writhing in pain; some of them never stopped screaming. The smell was sickening, and no one smiled. The hospital staff people were kind and professional, but they did not display any joy or humor.

After we left Heinz's room, I was escorted to an area where I could sit down and speak to the doctor. He was very kind, took my two hands in his and said how sorry he was.

"Your husband has third degree burns over 60% of his body. His lungs were damaged by the smoke and fumes that he inhaled. He is on oxygen right now, but if he is unable to breathe on his own, he will not survive. I have to be honest with you. I think his chances of survival are only 20%."

Immediately, I asked the doctor, "What can we do to improve those chances?"

"Mrs. Plutte, I am very sorry. We will do everything in our power to help your husband. We will begin skin grafts. This involves taking skin from the healthy parts of his body, like his buttocks and legs. Fortunately, he was wearing a leather belt that stopped the fire at around his waist. We will be able to use his skin rather than pig skin for the grafts. It will go much faster this way. Right now, it is very important to cover his exposed body as quickly as possible. He is constantly losing fluid the way it is right now. The skin grafting process requires that we change his dressing a few times a day, which is excruciatingly painful. Most people cannot bear that amount of pain. He will stay on the oxygen and we will test his lungs to see if they begin to heal. We need to take it one day at a time."

This was not what I expected to hear. I was stunned...and shocked. I couldn't believe the doctors thought there was such a poor chance that my husband would survive. The doctor was very kind, but his words were not reassuring at all. I sat there for a few minutes and then slowly made my way back to the waiting room where Janet was waiting. I knew she expected me to tell her what the doctor had said, but I just couldn't bring myself to tell her how bleak the doctor thought her father's prognosis was. I felt so helpless, because there was nothing I could do. I didn't want her to see how afraid I was, but I think she knew.

When we got home, Carol and Robert were also scared. "What happened at the hospital?" asked Carol. Again, I couldn't bring myself to tell them the truth, so I said, "Your father has a 50% chance of surviving, and we really need to pray for him."

Janet, Carol, and Robert were stunned to hear how bad the situation was—and they didn't even know the truth, that Heinz had only a 20% chance of surviving. We didn't really know how to pray, and it seemed wrong to start praying now that we needed God when we had basically ignored him up until this point. But we tried anyway, hoping God would hear us and help us in our hour of need.

The next days and weeks were excruciating. Janet did not go back to living at college on that Tuesday as she was supposed to. Instead, she started her classes, but she commuted back and forth to school because I was so upset, and she wanted to be with us. Carol and Robert went back to 10th and 9th grade respectively. I knew all three of my children wanted to stay with me, that they felt terrible leaving me at home, but I insisted they all go to school. Their education was important, and there was nothing they could do for their father or me anyway. I was blessed that my friends and neighbors were so good to me during that time, by taking me to the hospital to see Heinz and helping in other ways.

Carol's friend Lydia's mother Margaret drove me to the hospital on some days. Sometimes she waited in the cafeteria while I visited with Heinz, but some days, she even came with me to see him, if I asked her to. She let me decide what I wanted to do on any given day, and she was wonderfully kind and patient with me, which I will never forget. On other days, I took the bus and a train to the burn center, and our friend Günter, who worked in Philadelphia, would pick me up and drive me home on those days. Our friends Paula and Horst visited him a few times, too.

Most visits were very sad. Heinz talked only about how much pain he was in. When I arrived, he would immediately ask, "Anita, how can I get out of here? I can't stay here another day." On one visit when the children were with me, we realized that the bottom of his feet were not burned, so we began to rub them in an effort to show affection and hopefully alleviate some of his pain. With each visit, the doctors and nurses pulled me aside and explained what was happening with him. The news was never positive. One day, they told me he had gotten an infection. Another day, they told me they had discovered he was diabetic, too.

I went to the hospital every single day. At the beginning of the second week, I learned that Heinz was fighting with the doctors and nurses about changing the bandages, because it was so painful, he did not want them anymore. On one evening when Janet and Carol and I went to visit him, we noticed he looked so exhausted. Some of the swelling was gone, his face did not look so puffy, but his eyes were dark. The nurses explained that he had not been sleeping. They also told us he had fallen out of bed because he was trying to leave the hospital. "What can we do?" I asked.

"Well, we just continue on this course of the skin grafting, tending to his bandages, and testing his lungs. It will take a very long time. If he does survive, he will be here for months," said the nurse.

When the nurse walked away, Heinz said, "Janet, bring the car around. I need to get out of here."

I couldn't believe he really thought he could just go home, in the condition he was in. I told him, "Heinz, you have to stay here until you get better. You have to fight this, Heinz." I tried to stay calm, but I could feel I was beginning to breathe rapidly, and my chest was heaving. I hoped I would not have another panic attack, and I tried to regulate my breathing. I also didn't want Janet and Carol to see how upset I was.

"Anita, hide that cream so the nurse cannot find it. It is so painful, I just cannot stand it."

"Heinz, you have to try and cooperate with them, otherwise you will not get better," I said softly, but my hands were shaking, and I could feel my entire body was starting to tremble. Again, I tried to stay calm and regulate my breathing, but I could see Heinz was in so much pain—physically and emotionally, and it broke my heart to see him like this. Heinz just closed his eyes. I could see how my usually strong husband felt so defeated, so helpless. I didn't know what to do, or how I could make him feel better in any way. After a few minutes, I thought he had drifted off to sleep, so Carol and I left his room to get something to drink from the vending machine. Janet stayed behind, in case Heinz woke up: we didn't want him to think we had just left him without saying goodbye for the evening. She told me as soon as she was alone in the room with her father, she could tell he was trying to say something to her, but she could not hear him. She leaned over his bed and put her ear near his mouth.

He said, "Janet, I want you to unplug everything. I just want to die. You need to unplug everything while your mother is not here. I cannot take this pain anymore." She told me her first instinct was to obey him because for their entire lives, he had insisted that she and Carol and Robert obey him, no matter what the situation. But as she stood there, she realized that if she did what he asked, she would have that on her conscience for the rest of her life. She told me she was shaking: after all, she was only 17 years old. If she did what her father had asked her to do, she would leave behind the simplicity and innocence of childhood forever, all in a matter of five minutes.

She was sweating, and her heart was beating like a drum, because she was still so scared of her father. But she couldn't do what he asked, and she told him as gently as she could. "You know what, daddy? I can't do that. I do not want to be responsible for your death. I am sorry, but I cannot do what you are asking me." At this, she told me Heinz turned his head to look away from her, and raised his bandaged arm and waved it away from her. He said nothing, but Janet interpreted his silence and gestures as though he had said, "Ok, I am just done with you then."

When Carol and I returned to his room a few minutes later, Janet was sitting quietly in the far corner of his room. I wondered why she was not sitting beside his bed, but I didn't think to ask her why not. We stayed a few more minutes before we left to go home. I tried to reassure him: "Heinz, try to fight this. You are going to be able to do this, Heinz. I will come back tomorrow with Margaret."

As Janet drove us home, she didn't say anything. When I asked her why she was so quiet, she said only that she wasn't feeling well, that she felt sick to her stomach. It wasn't until many years later that

I learned what had happened in that hospital room while I was gone. Janet couldn't tell me at that time: she was overwhelmed by what her father had asked her to do, and she was still recovering from the shock of that encounter. I thought only that she was overcome by how poorly Heinz was doing; little did I know what a difficult decision my child had been asked to make that night. I wish I could have spared her that, just as I wish I could have spared my whole family from this ordeal, and I wish I could have helped Heinz in some way.

*****

The next day Margaret drove me back to the hospital. The doctors explained that his lungs were weak and he was not cooperating with them when they wanted to change bandages. Most of it was probably due to sleep deprivation, the doctor explained, but he was making their job very difficult. I did not know what to say or do. Margaret went in with me for a few minutes, and then she offered to wait in the cafeteria. "Anita, there is no rush. Take whatever time you need," she said.

Heinz was weaker than he had been the day before. Also, I could tell he was trying to tell me something. When I leaned over him, he said to me, "Anita, today I could FINALLY pray. I have not been able to think straight since I have been here. I have been in such pain and agony and I have hardly slept. But this morning, I could think clearly. I finally prayed." That was all he said. I thought this was so unusual, because Heinz and I did pray from time to time. I didn't really understand what he meant, but I hoped this was a good sign, that Heinz was hoping and praying to God that he would recover and get better.

Those two weeks that Heinz spent in the hospital were two weeks that I wish I did not have to live through. I was so grateful that we had friends like Paula and Horst, Günter and Elfriede, John and Theresa, Tante Else and Onkel Otto, Lydia's mother's Margaret, and my good neighbors to help me. At least I did not feel completely alone.

*****

A few hours later, that same evening, we got a call from the hospital. They would not tell us what happened, only that we needed to come down right away. I felt like I had been struck physically; I almost doubled over when I heard the nurse say we should come. Heinz had died, I just knew it, and why else would they call and tell us to come right away? I tried not to believe it, I didn't want to believe it, what would we do without Heinz? I said nothing to the children, only that we should go to the hospital, and I called Paula and Horst and asked them to drive us to the hospital. I needed our old friends to be with me, and they came and picked us up. The six of us drove to the hospital without a single word.

When we got there, it was around 10pm. Carol, Robert, Paula, and Horst waited outside while Janet and I went in to talk to the doctors. "I am very sorry, Mrs. Plutte. Your husband passed away earlier this evening. His lungs failed from the pneumonia. He had been in such agony from all the pain. I know this is a terrible time for you. He is free from the terrible pain he had been suffering. I am sure he is in a better place," said the doctor. He was a middle-aged man with a full head of completely gray hair. His face was not clean shaven; I wondered how long he had been in the hospital that day.

I was speechless. I did not say anything for a few minutes; I just couldn't. We looked at his body. It was the first time it was exposed to us from under the sheets. His shoulders looked like they had been chewed by some wild animal, like chunks of flesh had been bitten out of them. We could see his shoulder bones. We could see some of his organs. It was horrible, and heartbreaking, and shocking. No wonder he had been in such pain. My heart went out to him and the agony he had endured the last two weeks. Without a word, I covered him up again so the sheet covered his shoulders, and then I asked Janet to bring in Carol and Robert.

Words failed me in English, so I explained to them in German that their father was dead, and that I believed God had spared him further suffering and pain. I prayed and asked God to take care of him. None of us cried. We were all in such shock. No one said anything.

A few minutes later, Paula and Horst walked into the room. Paula saw Heinz lying motionless, and she cried out in pain: "Heinz, you cannot be dead!" She also spoke in German. Then she put her arms around me and hugged me and tried to comfort me. No more words were spoken.

A few minutes later, one of the doctors came in and asked if we would permit the hospital to do an autopsy. "I guess so," I said. I couldn't really think about that: I still couldn't believe Heinz was gone. It seemed like only a few days ago that we had celebrated such a beautiful, happy Christmas with all the children. I thought we had many more happy Christmases ahead of us. I had just turned 45 the week before. Our twenty-year wedding anniversary had been on January 19th, but Heinz and I had not been able to celebrate because of his accident. Now we never would. I was now a widow. And I had no idea what to do without Heinz. I honestly don't even remember the drive home that night, or anything that happened after. I must have gone to bed at some point, but I don't think I slept at all, even though I was exhausted with shock and grief.

*****

The next morning, I was awakened by knocking at our front door. It was Otto, who had married Heinz's Tante Else, after her husband Fritz had died a few years earlier. Otto was older than Else, but he always had a jolly sort of look about him. He was bald, with round glasses, and his face was always bright red. He was a beer drinker, and he had the gut to go along with it. That morning, though, Otto was very serious and intense.

I had not yet called anyone the night before, so I assumed Paula must have called him that morning. I wasn't really prepared to talk to anyone. In fact, I was still wearing the clothes I had worn the day before: I must have just fallen into bed. But I invited Otto in, and we sat down at the kitchen table. Mechanically, I began to make coffee. Janet, Carol, and Robert came in, too, and we all sat there, numb.

Otto said he wanted to help me compose the dreadful telegram that would inform everyone in Germany that Heinz had passed away. Right after Heinz had the accident, I had sent two telegrams to my Mama and Heinz's father telling them what had happened. Otto knew I would need to contact them again, now that Heinz was dead.

"Anita, I will help you write these telegrams and I want to pay for them," he said. I did not know how to respond. I really had no idea where to begin, to make all the arrangements I knew needed to be made. Otto dictated the telegram in German and asked Janet to write it down. It said simply, "Last night, Heinz went to sleep forever." He repeated it several times and insisted that Janet read it back to him to make sure she had gotten it right. "Ok, then," he said, "let's call them up and dictate it to the operator." He did this and read off the two addresses, one to my Mama, and the other to Heinz's father, as I had just done a few weeks ago. I couldn't believe it was just two weeks ago. It took about twenty minutes because Otto had to spell each word for the operator, and he wanted to make sure the addresses were accurate. "I hope they got my first telegram about the accident. Otherwise, they are going to be completely shocked," I said, suddenly remembering how poor even the telegram service was in East Germany. I could only hope.

Otto then offered to help us with the funeral arrangements. "Do you want me to call the funeral home, Anita?" he asked.

"Otto, I think the children and I can do this ourselves," I said very calmly and evenly, "But thank you so much for coming over, Otto." I knew he meant well and wanted to help, but I just wanted to be alone with my children.

After Otto left, I asked Janet to call Pastor Kuehn at Feltonville Lutheran Church. We went to church only a few times a year, but it was still the church we considered ourselves a part of, and it was the church where Heinz and I had been married. Pastor Kuehn had also confirmed Janet, Carol, and Robert. Janet spoke to Pastor Kuehn, and he promised to come over that afternoon. He suggested we call the Welsch Funeral Home, so Janet made that call, too; the funeral director also promised to come over that afternoon. While Janet made these calls, I just sat at the kitchen table. I couldn't bear to talk to anyone, so when Janet asked whether it was OK if the pastor and the funeral director came to the house that afternoon; all I could do was nod. I was mute with shock and grief.

Later in the day, Pastor Kuehn came over. He was a bald middle-aged man with black round glasses. I was still sitting at the kitchen table when Janet answered the door and invited him in. He talked about the funeral and how he would handle it. "Anita, often at these funerals, everybody buys so many flowers. If you don't want that, we could say that, in lieu of flowers, you would like everyone to make a donation to the church or to a charity in Heinz's honor," he said. I told him that would be fine. I still felt numb, and I didn't really care whether there were flowers or not. I couldn't believe I was planning my husband's funeral.

Right after Pastor Kuehn left, the funeral director, Mr. Welsch, came in. He was a young man, probably in his early 30s. He wore a black coat, a black suit, a black tie, and black shoes. Only his shirt was white. He carried a folder of papers. Mr. Welsch also sat at our kitchen table and got right down to business. I asked Janet, Carol, and Robert to sit with me to discuss the funeral arrangements: I needed their help, and it was important to me that they are comfortable with all the decisions we would need to make.

First, we had to choose the day of the funeral, which Mr. Welsch then confirmed by calling Pastor Kuehn. Then Mr. Welsch asked me to pick out a casket. "Well, we have to have a closed casket since Heinz's body was so badly burned. I do not know which one to choose," I said.

"Well, I think this casket of all natural wood might be appropriate for Heinz since he was a carpenter," suggested Mr. Welsch. He showed us a nice-looking casket made of light-colored wood. "Yes, I think Heinz would approve of that," I told him. "Also, I would like to put some pictures of our family and Heinz's father in the casket with him. Would that be OK?"

Mr. Welsch said it would be fine, and Janet said she thought this was a wonderful idea, one that would please all of us. Later, Janet told me she was surprised that I had even thought of this idea. I don't know why I did, I just knew I wanted us to be with Heinz forever, in any way we could.

Mr. Welsch also suggested that we order flowers, one bouquet from me and one from the children. I agreed, and Janet again called the florist to place the order. I don't know what I would have done without my Janet that day; she was so strong and capable. I hoped we could all be strong in the days and years ahead.

*****

"When I was woven together in the depths of the earth, your eyes saw my unformed body. All the days ordained for me were written in your book before one of them came to be." Psalm 139:15-16

—14—

The Funeral

The night before the funeral, I was completely petrified just thinking about the funeral and how I would make it through the day. My emotions were so intense. I just didn't want to live through that day. The fear and the emotional pain were completely overwhelming and I didn't believe that I could go through it without completely falling apart. My legs barely held my weight as I stumbled into my bed the night before that dreaded day. I was exhausted. I was empty. More than ever, I missed my family back in East Germany. I really had no real family here, only my kids. We did have wonderful friends, and I was thankful for them. Still, on that day, I felt very alone. I was so heartsick over the way Heinz had suffered for those two weeks. I wished he would have died right away and been spared all that pain.

I tossed and turned in my bed all night. I looked at Heinz's U.S. Army picture on the wall. He was so handsome. I knew he had tried to provide a good home for us. Why did he have to die like that? At 1am, I got up to go to the bathroom. I felt so weak. My head was one large headache. By 1:30am, I walked down to the kitchen and took some aspirin and drank a glass of water. I just sat at the kitchen table and could not even move. I heard the dog crying from the basement, but I did not let him come upstairs. What was I going to do? I felt so terrible for the children. They were looking to me, and I felt weak.

I went back up to bed around 2am and lay in my bed shaking. I was just so afraid to go through the day ahead. I was not sure I could keep myself together. I wanted to be strong for the kids. Frightened is not even adequate to describe how I felt. I kept praying to God that He would help me get through the day. I prayed for strength.

I never really fell asleep. When I saw that is was 6am, I just decided to walk downstairs. I took some more aspirin. I felt so empty. I sat at the table again and looked around our home. I just did not believe that I could go on.

A little while later, much to my great and overwhelming surprise, I began to experience a feeling of complete peace. I could not explain it. It flooded my mind. It felt as though someone had picked me up by the arms and was carrying me. My enormous fear of having to make it through this day was gone. This feeling of peace I had was so powerful. I was unable to even describe it to my kids. Although I didn't understand it, I was just happy to accept the peace I felt.

The black limousine pulled up to our house on Medway Road early in the morning as promised. It was a very cold February day: Friday, February 4, 1977. The sky was clear, but it was windy. The funeral director helped me get into the car. Janet, Carol, and Robert followed. The pastor had met us at the house, and he too rode in the limousine with our family. No one spoke at first. The ride to the Lutheran church normally took about 40 minutes, but that day, it seemed much longer. On the way over, Pastor Kuehn spoke of the death of his teenage son, who had been killed in a car accident a few years ago. "No one really knows why God allows things. We just have to accept both the good and the bad." To be honest, his words did not really offer me much comfort at the time, but I guess that was what pastors were supposed to say.

When we arrived at the church, we were escorted to the front of the church by the funeral director. People came down the center aisle to tell me how sorry they were. Horst, Paula, Elfriede, and Günter sat right behind me. One by one, friends and neighbors came over to me. Some people who knew Heinz from work, who I never met before came too. It was actually nice to hear a brief word from them about what they remembered and appreciated about Heinz. Almost everyone was crying by the time they got to me – I found myself trying to comfort them with the strength I seem to have miraculously received that morning. I listened attentively as Pastor Kuehn spoke. I wanted to believe that Heinz had made it to Heaven, but how could anyone know for sure? I was glad that his suffering was over. When the funeral was over, Heinz's casket was carried out of the church. I had asked friends and family to be Heinz's pallbearers: Otto, Horst, Günter, John, Joachim (one of Heinz's friends), and

Billy (Wilhelm's son; Onkel Wilhelm had died about 10 years earlier). I thought Heinz would approve.

For days and weeks after the funeral, I kept having dreams about Heinz. I saw him sitting in the Volkswagen (a car we had traded in three years before), in front of the garage, with bandages around his entire body and his head. It was so disturbing. I had the same dream over and over. I prayed and prayed for comfort and relief from those dreams. Life was hard enough when I was awake and it felt like torture not to be able to escape my pain even in my dreams.

Then I had one last dream about Heinz, and it was very different. He was standing behind some of the tall trees at the German club, the club where we had often attended social events with our friends. In this dream, Heinz looked completely fine. He was wearing the suit that we had him buried in. He waved to me and smiled at me from the distance. It was like he was telling me he was fine. After that dream, I never had any of the other disturbing dreams again.

*****

"But if from there you seek the Lord your God, you will find him, if you look for him with all your heart and will all your soul." Deuteronomy 4:29

—15—

Putting Our Lives Back Together

In the days and weeks that followed the funeral, I realized that Heinz had actually tied up a lot of loose ends in his life before his death. It was almost eerie, like he had some premonition that he could not put into words. We had traveled to Germany a year and a half before his death where he was able to enjoy special time and interaction with his father. He retraced the steps he had taken so many years earlier, when he had escaped East Germany and fled to West Germany, and he had introduced me to many of the people I had only heard about but had never met. These people had helped Heinz along his journey to America, and he was pleased he had had the opportunity to tell them that he had made it to the United States and that his dream of a better life had become a reality. He was glad he could thank them all for their help – something he had wanted to do for over 20 years.

Heinz had also created a wonderful last Christmas for our family, although at the time, we did not know it would be our last

Christmas together. I believe the gifts he purchased for Janet, Carol, and Robert—the first time he had ever really asked them what they wanted, and the first time he had gone out and bought the gifts himself—were his way of trying to tell his children how much he loved them. For whatever reason, he couldn't express his love and pride in our children in words, but I believe this was his way of trying to make amends. During that season, I remember wondering why he was being so generous; we didn't have any more money than in other years.

*****

The day after the funeral, Lydia's mother Margaret came over with a few bags of groceries, and she helped me put them away. Then we sat in the kitchen and talked for a long time. She was and still is such a sensitive person. She was trying to comfort me, and she offered us whatever help we needed. She knew that eventually, Janet would move back to her dorm at the University of Pennsylvania, and even though we twould have two cars, no one would be able to drive them. Carol was still only 15, and she wouldn't turn 16 until the summer, at which point she could get her learner's permit. But until then, unless Janet was home, we would need rides to get wherever we needed to go. Lydia's mother told me she would drive us anytime we needed her.

A few days later, I called the Carpenters' Union to see what benefits our family was entitled to; I thought Heinz would at least be entitled to a pension. I never would have believed what the man told me. "I am very sorry," he said icily, not sounding sorry at all, "but your husband was five days short of his 20 years, so you and your children are not entitled to anything at all." I felt like someone had just punched me. But there was nothing I could do. What would we do for money?

*****

About a week after the funeral, Janet went back to college, so Carol helped me open all the cards we had received. There was a large pile of them, and none of us had had the energy to even look at them before. We sat in the living room, on the sofa, and Carol opened each card and read it and then passed it to me. Each card included a very nice note or word of encouragement, and almost everyone had given us money. Only one or two people had made a donation to the church. Janet's high-school friends had made a donation to the Burn Center. I was surprised that people had given us money, since I had not told anyone other than Günter and Paula that we would not be entitled to a pension from Heinz's union. After we opened all the cards, Carol told me we had been given more than $2,000. I could not believe how generous everyone was: $2,000 was a lot of money in 1977! By comparison, our monthly mortgage payment on our house was only about $100.

A few days later, around the middle of February, Carol came in to the kitchen while I was eating breakfast. She was carrying a small box, wrapped as a present, and she approached me somewhat tentatively.

"Mom," she said gently, "Here is a present daddy bought for you for your 20-year anniversary. He gave it to me after Christmas, to hide in my room and wrap it; he was going to give it to you on January 19th, when he got home from work, but...he..." her voice trailed off, as she couldn't bear to remind me the he was already in the burn center then. "Anyway," she resumed, "do you want to open it now?"

She handed me the box and without a word, I slowly removed the beautiful blue ribbon. From the shape of the box, I knew it was some sort of jewelry. Gingerly, I lifted the lid – this would be the very last gift from my beloved Heinz. When I saw the sparkling watch inside, I started to cry, at first softly and then much harder, until I was sobbing. It was a simple yet elegant gold watch, with an oval face surrounded by small diamonds. I was crying so hard, I could not really speak, so Carol said, "that was really nice of dad to buy you such an expensive watch for your anniversary."

"It is beautiful," I agreed. "He must have chosen this one with diamonds, since I never got any diamonds in my engagement ring." I could see Heinz had taken great care to choose something he knew I would like, and would use, and I started to cry again. I couldn't believe he wasn't here to give it to me himself. I couldn't believe we celebrated our 20th wedding anniversary around his hospital bed with a cake from the nursing staff, and that we would never celebrate another. I couldn't believe Heinz was gone, and I wouldn't be able to thank him for such a lovely gift.

"I had no idea about this watch," I told Carol. "I never even told him that I wanted anything for our anniversary. I will always treasure this."

I still wear that watch every day, and whenever I look at it, I think of Heinz, the boy I met at the dancing school and the man I married, not the husband I buried too soon. This watch was his message of love for me, even if the words were never spoken.

*****

A few days later, an insurance agent came by. I didn't know what he wanted, so I sent him away. I just closed the door in his face. When I told Carol about it, though, she told me he was probably bringing Heinz's life insurance check. She said, "Don't send him away, mom. We need that money." And she called the company and explained our situation, and asked if the man could come back with the check. My 15-year-old daughter was mature even before her father had died; in the weeks and months ahead, I would learn how capable all my children were: they were so strong, and we all helped each other get through that dark and difficult time. The insurance agent came back the next day, and we received the check: it was for several thousand dollars, but a good bit of it was needed to pay the remaining hospital bills and for the funeral. Still, we were glad to have it.

After a few more days, Margaret drove me over to the Social Security office. The monthly benefit was very modest, but we thought it would be enough to pay all of our bills if we were very careful. Janet's monthly benefit was to be used for her room and board at University of Pennsylvania, and Robert's and Carol's benefits would come in my name until they turned 18. My children were so wonderful: they wanted to do all they could to help support us. I felt so helpless: I didn't have a job, I couldn't drive, and I had no idea what to do. I was afraid we would lose the house. And if that happened, I didn't know where we would go.

Then, out of the blue, I got a call from a friend of one of our friends from the German club. "My name is Rick Sullivan, and I heard about your situation. I am terribly sorry. How much do you have in unpaid medical bills, not covered by the insurance?" he asked.

"Oh, I really don't know yet, but it is at several thousand dollars," I told him.

"You know, these doctors and hospitals assume there is a huge life insurance policy, and they just figure you can pay for it with the money from insurance. If it is OK with you, I will call all these doctors and hospitals and see what I can do," he said.

I agreed to let him come over, and I shared all the bills and contact names with him. He took notes, but he did not keep any of our documents. I was worried that nothing would come of his visit, but I appreciated the fact that he wanted to help. So I was stunned when he called back only a few days later. "Anita, don't pay any of those bills. The doctors and hospitals agreed to cut the amount you owe in half. The hospital says you can pay as much as you are able each month until the bill is paid off. They won't charge you interest. Wait for the new statements, and don't do anything until you receive them," he said. I couldn't believe he had been able to help us with Heinz's bills! I made payments to the doctors and hospitals for many years until everything was paid off. Sometimes, I was able to pay only $10 a month, but I was so grateful that he had made these arrangements for us, and I was relieved when those bills were finally paid in full.

*****

A few weeks later, Janet and Carol helped me figure out how we were going to do everything that Heinz had done for us. Carol called the banks, and I learned how to pay the bills for the very first time. Carol helped me get everything set up: she was excellent in math, and she was very organized. When she found Heinz's checkbook, she noticed he had a piece of paper in it, with the English spelling of all the numbers: 1-10 and then 20, 30, 40, and so on. It was in Carol's handwriting, and when she showed it to me, she said she remembered writing it out for Heinz when she was in the third grade. "I can't believe he kept this in his checkbook all these years. I guess he never really learned to spell the numbers. I wonder why he never asked Janet to do it—she was the smart one," she said.

While Carol sorted through all the paperwork, Janet went through Heinz's closet. She suggested we give some of his personal belongings to Robert, including a nice watch, and I agreed. We mailed Heinz's other watch to his brother, Winfried. Then we packed up and shipped most of his clothes to his father, Paul. The rest we donated to Goodwill.

*****

Then about two months after Heinz died, his friend Franz offered to come over and help us clean out the garage. Franz was a German man Heinz had worked with. He and his wife, Hildegard, were at least ten years older than we were. Hildegard had often tried to teach me how to sew my own clothes. I never really liked to sew, so Hildegard and I had little in common. As a result, we did not see Franz and Hildegard that much, not socially. But I thought it was kind of Franz to offer to help, and he spent a few hours cleaning out the garage. Then he came back into the house to say good-bye to me and to wish us all well.

After he drove away, Carol mentioned that Franz had loaded his truck with many of her father's tools, so she asked me, "Did you let him have those tools, mom?"

"Well, he helped me clean up the garage, and I don't know what to do with them, so I didn't see the harm in him taking them."

Carol was annoyed, though, and she told me so: "Well, mom, you could have saved them for Robert. I bet that man took daddy's best tools. You didn't need him to do anything. He probably just offered to help so he could take his tools."

"It doesn't matter, Carol, the trash is out of the garage, and I wanted him to have something for it." I didn't want to argue with Carol, and I didn't want to believe that someone would really take advantage of us after Heinz's death. Carol was probably right, though, because we never saw or heard from Franz again.

*****

A few weeks later, I received a letter from my Mama and learned that the first telegram I had sent to Germany, informing her of Heinz's accident, had arrived much later than the second telegram, which told her Heinz had died. I realized if this is how my Mama had found out, then the same thing had probably happened to Heinz's father, so Paul probably had had no warning when that second telegram arrived. Everyone was so shocked. This upset me so much. Communication with our families had always been frustrating because phone calls to East Germany were not yet permitted, but to find out so suddenly that a loved one had died was especially upsetting: I felt so awful for Paul and Marta and Winfried and Christa. Soon after, I received so many letters expressing sorrow, from my sisters and brothers, from Heinz's family, and from other friends in Germany.

*****

With Janet away at college, when we needed something during the week, Margaret or one of the neighbors took us food shopping. Janet came home most weekends to help out. Carol was close to turning 16, and I knew she could not wait to drive. We did not want to depend on other people to get us places. As soon as she turned 16 in July, Paula's niece Inge drove her to get her learner's permit. She passed and took a driving course right away, and after only two weeks, she got her license. Janet was using Heinz's car, so Carol drove our other car, the blue Dodge Dart that I used to drive and that Janet had her accident in. That was only a year ago, but it seemed like it was only yesterday that I talked Heinz out of yelling at Janet for hitting the telephone pole, yet in the year that had elapsed and since Heinz had died, our lives had changed so much. Sometimes, I could not believe what had happened. For months after the accident and funeral, I felt paralyzed. I got up every morning, and I went through the motions of getting Carol and Robert off to school, but

I felt as though I was sleepwalking. I knew the kids were worried about me, but I didn't know what to do or how to cope.

At the same time, my Mama wrote to tell us she had decided to come to Philadelphia to spend some time with us. Below are some of the letters she sent right before her trip:

14.7.77

Dear Anita and dear children,

So you don't have to wait too long, I am going to send you a few short lines. This morning I saw your Papa and he told me that he sent you two packages, and so he and I thank you very much for the items Onkel Otto brought along. We will talk about everything when I come and visit you. We were very happy, however ??? You know my dearest what I mean. Yes, the time is getting closer and closer and I am sure you got the last letter when I told you the time and the dates and I am going to tell you again. The time is the same, but I put a little note in there with the departure and arrival times. Around noon time, I am in Prague and about 5 in the evening I will be in NY. I am just writing you all this information again, because it is possible some of the letters might not reach you.

Friday morning, I will go to Karl Marx Stadt and Renate and I will send a package to send to you. My dear Robert, I almost break my head, what can I bring for you? So many things I cannot take along and it is really hurtful to me and I do not know what to bring. And dear Anita, in the next few days, I will have to deal with the fuel that I have to store. And then you have to throw it through the window into the basement. The big washing house – I finished it.

However, my little garden still needs some tweaking. And then I have only one more week left. And then I have to compose myself, get my hair done, and prepare myself for my big trip which will take me to you my dear children. Onkel Otto told me how much all of you are looking forward to my arrival. I can hardly wait. Looking forward to our reunion. I kiss you with a hopeful heart. Your Mama. Many greetings to everybody. Karli visited me on Tuesday and he would love it if he could come with me also.

19.7.77

My dear Anita,

Yesterday I came back from Renate and we packed the package for you. Some things are from me, some things are from Renate and Hans and Papa wanted to contribute to it also. The cost for the plane ticket, I want to pay all by myself. Papa also sent a package to your kids. I found something for Robert. I think I am going to bring him an army knife along. You told me that he lost one. I am sure he will be happy since he lost his old one. My dear Anita, I am really happy that you all had a few days of vacation, and I was happy that those people invited you to their homes. I hope it was peaceful and a distraction. I am glad that you have good friends over there and it makes me feel better to know that. They must be nice, and it is nice when you have someone there who you can get advice from or who can do things that Heinz could have done if he had lived. I think I wrote to you already that Otto was here and I was thanking you already for everything that he brought along. I am so glad that my children all turned out to be honest, responsible people and I raised them that way and I didn't ask for anything when I was in dire need and I am proud that I accomplished that.

My Anita, the name of the airline — I do not know yet, we will find out. And the exit in NY, I am sure I will find that too. And I am sure that I will see you then. I will be so happy when the trip is behind me and I can just embrace you in my arms. With many heartfelt greeting and kisses for you, Your Mama

My Mama arrived from Germany in August 1977; seven months after Heinz died, and stayed with us for three months. She shared my room, and we stayed up many nights just talking and crying. It was wonderful therapy for me to have my own Mama with us.

When she finally arrived, we were so happy, and we all enjoyed her company so much. And she wanted to help with the household chores, but she wasn't familiar with our American conveniences. One day, when Carol came home from school, she found her grandmother in tears. She could not imagine what her grandmother was crying about. Then my Mama held up a pair of Carol's purple pants, and Carol saw that my Mama had burned them by leaving the iron on them for too long. Carol told her she did not care, but my Mama still felt so bad and would not stop crying.

Every afternoon, my Mama sat at our kitchen table and drank a glass of beer with two spoons of sugar dissolved in it. When she finished the beer, she took a paper towel and wiped the glass out. Then she used that wet paper towel to wipe the leaves all of our houseplants. We all thought it was very strange, but we let her do it anyway. What was most important was that she was here with us: she was salve for my pain, and I believe the children also benefited from the time she spent with us.

Here are some of her diary entries from her three-month stay with us:

15.8.77

In the morning we went to the cemetery and visited Heinz's grave. It is very sad. You cannot even believe that Heinz is lying under the surface of the earth...

18.8.77

Today Anita cut the grass, Robert baked a cake and I hung out in the garden. Janet went to a birthday party; however, somebody stole her pocketbook. All of us were very upset. Otto and Else came for a visit and we talked about everything.

28.8.77

After we had breakfast, we drove to Feltonville Lutheran Church for the German service. It was very spiritual, but it was also very scary for me because I saw Heinz's coffin in front of the altar. I saw it very clearly before me. Anita told me 80 people attended his funeral service and 21 cars went along to the cemetery. It must have been truly devastating. And of top of it, it was brutally cold the day of his funeral.

2.9.77

Today the children took me to the Franklin Institute. We marched through the heart and the lung, exactly the way the blood flows through the body. In one of those rooms we saw ships, airplanes and trains. Then I learned how to manufacture paper. Then we saw the lunar module. Everything was interesting. We also learned a lot about energy and we could test ourselves. It was a fantastic day.

13.9.77

Today we had to clean the snack bar, where Carol worked during the entire summer. We all helped her get the place clean. She earned some nice money during the summer; however, the poor thing had to sweat so much, because the summer was so hot.

25.9.77

Günter and Elfriede came to visit us and they showed us movies of when Anita's children were small. I never had the privilege to see that. In the evening, Günter drove us to a big stadium in Philadelphia to see ice hockey. Philadelphia vs. New York. New York won 4-3. You should see that stadium. I never saw anything like it. It seats 17,000 people. And I found out that they sold 17,070 tickets. You should have seen me. I was really cheering for Philadelphia.

15.10.77

We went to the cemetery today and saw Heinz's grave again. It is always a very sad time. When you stand in front of the grave, you think about the good Heinz. The dear Anita bought a beautiful grave stone. There was a small area to plant some flowers. The cemeteries are so different here than what we are used to in Frohburg.

25.10.77

At 11 o'clock in the morning, we met Tante Else in center city of Philadelphia. We drove again through this beautiful park, Fairmount Park. It was a beautiful day. The trees were colorful and majestic. Afterwards we had lunch "Lunsch" in a restaurant located in a mall. You could buy everything there. We ate fish with noodles and green beans and of course, one cup of coffee.

Everything was delicious. The dining room was big and beautiful. There were carpeted walls. Unbelievable. Afterwards, we went back and visited City Hall and saw the statue of William Penn. And oh, these enormous skyscrapers. However, where Anita lives with her children, she lives in a beautiful area in northeast Philadelphia and I am happy that she has that house. Now it is getting closer to the time I have to leave. We filled out the luggage tags when we got home. I cannot even think about having to say good-bye. It is just too painful.

*****

"They will neither hunger nor thirst, nor will the desert heat or the sun beat upon them. He who has compassion on them will guide them and lead them beside springs of water." Isaiah 49:10

—16—

Graduating from College

When my Mama left in the fall of 1977, I still had no idea what to do. And Carol was increasingly worried about our financial situation. "Mom, you have to do something soon, the Social Security won't last forever. Once I go to college, we'll have only my Social Security. Robert's will stop if he doesn't continue his education," Carol pleaded. It was true. The money was going to run out soon, and Robert did not want to go to college. He had gotten a job at McDonald's, and he was happy doing that at the time. Robert gave me most of the money he earned to help pay the bills. Carol and Janet also gave me most of their earnings from their summer and part-time jobs.

Carol asked her 11th grade history teacher if he had any suggestions on career possibilities for me. He suggested I become a court stenographer because it was lucrative, he said, and the schooling would take only about two years. I appreciated the suggestion, and I know he wanted to help. But I wasn't sure that was something I would be good at or enjoy doing, so I didn't look into that further. I also didn't want to go back to working in a kitchen somewhere, either at a restaurant or a school, because even though I liked to cook, I wanted to do something more with my life, and I needed to earn more than a minimum-wage job would pay me. I knew I needed to do something soon. How ironic, that all those years when I had wanted a job and begged Heinz to let me get one—if only he had, I wouldn't have faced such a difficult situation after he died.

Other people also had ideas on what we should do to ease our financial situation. One day, a man who worked in the kitchen at our German club came over. His name was Wolfgang, and Heinz had been friends with him. Wolfgang was a heavy, middle-aged man, and he walked with a limp. I invited him in and directed him to the kitchen table. I made him a cup of coffee and then I asked, "So, Wolfgang, what brings you here today?"

"Well, Anita, there is a man at the club, Helmut, you know him. His wife died of cancer a few years ago. He is a nice man. He has a nine-year-old daughter. He is lonely. He needs someone to cook and clean for him. Maybe you can come over to the club to talk to him. He knows you. He remembers you, and maybe if he likes you, he will marry you."

"How insulting," I thought, but at the same time, I realized that in Wolfgang's mind, he was doing something nice. That was the culture of my generation. A woman meant nothing unless she was associated with a man. I got up and walked toward my stove at the back of the kitchen, so he wouldn't be able to see my face while I spent a few minutes composing my thoughts. Even though I tried not to be blunt, the truth just spilled out: "Wolfgang, thank you very much, but I have no intention of ever getting married again. Once was enough. I am going to get an education, and I will be fine. Please tell Helmut that I am not interested, and please do not suggest something like this ever again." That was really bold for me. But I wasn't going to marry anybody just so that he could take care of me and I could cook and clean for him.

Janet and Carol had already been encouraging me to go to college. I had not realized how much I wanted to do that until I had that conversation with Wolfgang. I talked to the girls again the next day. Janet was now in her sophomore year of college and Carol was a junior in high school.

"You know, mom, why don't you just go to college and do something that you really like?" Janet said. "You still have time. Carol will get Social Security until she graduates from college, and Robert wants to keep working at McDonalds anyway. In the meantime, figure out what you want to do, and just go for it."

The words washed over me and calmed me. *Yes,* I thought, *this makes sense*. I recalled the years that my Mama was so dependent on me when my Papa was not around. I could understand how much she must have hated being in that situation. I did not want to be a burden on or dependent on my kids either.

So in January of 1978, only a year after Heinz died, I started a program at the local community college for people who want to get an education but haven't been in school for a while. I actually needed to take many basic math classes before I could even enter college. I remember speaking to the counselor one day when she asked me, "What would you like to do, Anita?"

"Well, I have always been interested in the medical profession. But I don't have four years now. I have to start working soon, or I will have to sell my house," I said.

"Well, why don't you become a medical lab technician?" she said. The counselor discussed many options with me, but the idea of being an MLT intrigued me. It was a two-year program with good prospects for getting a job. I pondered the advice from the counselor, and I decided to go ahead with that program. I felt completely at peace about the decision.

*****

I started Philadelphia Community College's Act Now Program (a prerequisite for college curriculum) in the spring of 1978. Within months of starting school, our phone rang constantly. Robert usually answered it, but it was almost always for me. He couldn't believe how many calls I got, and he couldn't believe who was calling me: "It sounds like a 20-year-old kid; he says his name is John," he would tell me. Many of the boys in my classes called me when they were upset about their girlfriends and were looking for advice.

On weekends, I socialized with my fellow college students. "Carol and Robert, I am going into the city to meet these kids for lunch, and then we are going to the Franklin Institute. Afterwards, they will drive me home," I told them one day. They stared at me in disbelief, but I know they were also happy I was making new friends—regardless of how young they were!—and they were happy that I was going out and doing something, instead of just sitting home and being depressed. After that, there were many Saturday nights when Carol and Robert would make popcorn and snuggle up under blankets to watch the Philadelphia Flyers game while I prepared to go out. And that first Christmas that I was in school, I invited some of my new friends to our home to celebrate a German Christmas. They all enjoyed the German pyramide, the nutcrackers from the Erzgebirge region of Germany, and the cookies and cakes I had made. At the end of the night, I was so happy when everyone walked out with small tins of Christmas cookies and chocolate treats.

At the same time, Carol was about to graduate from high school and enter college. She had decided to major in accounting because the job prospects were good. She feared that I might not get a job when I graduated and she was certain she could pay our bills with an accounting job. When she started college that fall, I officially started my two-year college course curriculum to become a medical lab technician. Carol lived at home and commuted to a local

Philadelphia college, so that her monthly Social Security check (which now came in her own name) could also be used to pay our bills. She also realized we were entitled to Veteran's benefits because Heinz had served in the U.S. Army. Between earnings from Janet's and Carol's summer and part-time jobs, Robert's job, and the Social Security and Veteran's benefits, we kept up with the bills. When Robert graduated from high school, he chose not to go to college and he began to work more hours at McDonald's, sometimes up to 50 hours a week. I worried that he didn't go to college, but he seemed happy in what he was doing, so I hoped that he might go later in life.

In 1981, four-and-a-half years after Heinz died; I completed the Act Now program, the prerequisite courses, and the two-year associate's degree courses. I was 49 years old when I passed the state exam and became a licensed medical lab technician. Along the way, I made many friends. These new friendships and my studies helped me to focus on my goals and the future—I didn't have time to dwell on the past.

The same year I graduated from college, Carol completed her sophomore year of college. Janet had graduated from the University of Pennsylvania a year and a half earlier and had started her career as a biochemist. To celebrate all of our achievements, we decided to have a party at our house on Medway Road, and we invited many of my new and old friends and many of our neighbors.

At the celebration, I told my children, "I realized that my life had circled around. I remember when I was a young girl in Germany, and I had to shovel potatoes and bring home extra food from the deli to help my Mama feed my sisters and brothers. I felt as though that's what you three were doing for me. You were working and handing over your checks so I could pay the bills. I have hated this and I was so determined not to hold you back. I wanted you three children to be proud of me."

"Other than becoming a mother, this day is probably the most exciting day of my entire life," I told them. My kids said I was glowing. I *was* proud of what I had accomplished. And I wore my black cap and gown all day.

A few weeks later, I started my new career at a local hospital. At first, I was hired for various shifts in the lab, but eventually, I was offered a daytime position in microbiology. I was thrilled to have gotten this position and I really enjoyed it. Still, after those driving incidents, I never wanted to get behind the wheel of a car again. Occasionally it was Robert, but mostly it was Carol who drove me to and from the hospital. She often drove me on her way to or from the local college that she commuted to.

Even though I had been in America for 25 years, I continued to have a very thick German accent. When Carol would call me at the hospital to confirm transportation, she would often tease me by disguising her voice and asking, "May I schpeak to the Vomann vitt dah Germann ahksent?" One time, Carol called me at work and someone else answered. Carol didn't realize that it wasn't me who answered when she started to ask for the "Woman with the German Accent" with her disguised voice. Of course, the person knew exactly who the call was for, but Carol and I were both completely embarrassed. After we got over the initial embarrassment, we both laughed hysterically. As we told the story to Janet and Robert, they too could not stop laughing over the situation. Despite all we had been through, I was so grateful that we still had a sense of humor and we could laugh about things. Before long, they all started to call me "The Woman with the German accent", which was later shortened to "THE WOMAN" or "WOMAN". As Janet, Carol and Robert got married, their spouses naturally wondered about the strange name that they called their mother. After hearing the story and having a good laugh, they quickly adopted the same name for me. It only changed after my grandchildren came along and every started to call me 'Oma' (which means Grandma in German) but I do still hear "Woman" once in a while.

*****

I worked at the hospital for eleven years, until my knees yielded to degenerative arthritis, and I had to have both knees replaced. I was 60 years old when I retired, which was sooner than I wanted to, but I had a career that I am very proud of. And I made wonderful friends with many of my co-workers, friendships I still enjoy and treasure.

*****

"The fear of the Lord is the beginning of wisdom, and knowledge of the Holy One is understanding." Proverbs 9:10

Heinz's U.S. Army picture: He served during the Korean War which ended in 1953.

Heinz's funeral in February 1977: The funeral director, me, Paula, Janet, Horst, Robert, and Carol. Despite my anxiety about the funeral the night before, I was miraculously calm and able to get through that difficult day.

My Mama and me at Heinz's grave: The stone was placed on the grave several months after the funeral. The stone reads "Der Herr ist mein Hirte", which means "the Lord is my shepherd". My Mama came and stayed with our family for three months in the same year that Heinz died.

Graduation day for me, in 1981, at age 49! I was so happy to get my Associate's Degree and begin my new career as a medical lab technician.

PART IV

WE WERE NEVER ALONE

—17—

Finding God

After Heinz died, Janet got more involved in activities on the campus of University of Pennsylvania. She told me that she was involved in many Christian organizations on the campus. I told her I thought it was great!

What Janet was trying to tell me is that she had found God, and that she had a personal relationship with Jesus. She told me it took her a while to realize that she needed to become a Christian because she had always thought we were Christians. And so did I! After all, we went to church and sang religious songs. We celebrated Christmas and Easter. The children had been baptized as babies, and they all celebrated their confirmations when they turned 14. During their confirmation preparations, they went to church often. Granted after Robert was confirmed our attendance at church dropped to Christmas and Easter. **Still, what was the difference?**

My pride kept me from accepting what my daughter was trying to say. And I continued to believe that if a person was basically good, that he or she would go to heaven. And of course, I always believed in God.

Janet and later her husband, Bob explained to me that in order to become a Christian, a person first has to recognize that they are separated from God because of their sin. Janet said this was not so easy for her to admit because she had spent her whole life up to that point trying to be perfect, in order to please her father. *["There is no one righteous, not even one; there is no one who understands, no one who seeks God. All have turned away; they have together become worthless there is no one who does good, not even one." Romans 3:10].*

To become a Christian, a person also has to believe that Jesus was the son of God who came to earth to pay for our sins so that we can be right with God. Without Jesus, our sin separates us from God. *["But now a righteousness from God, apart from law, has been made known to which the Law and the Prophets testify. This righteousness from God comes through <u>faith in Jesus Christ to all who believe</u>. There is no difference, for <u>all have sinned and fall short of the glory of God</u>, and are justified freely by his grace through the redemption that came by Christ Jesus. God presented him as a sacrifice of atonement through faith in his blood." Romans 3: 21-25.]*

Finally, to become a Christian, a person needs to ask Him to forgive them of their sins and enter into their life and show them how to live differently. *["...That if you <u>confess with your mouth</u>, "Jesus is Lord," and <u>believe in your heart</u> that God raised him from the* *dead, you will be saved. For it is with your heart that you believe and are justified and it is with your mouth that you confess and are saved." Romans 10:9-10].* Once that happens, Jesus by the Holy Spirit somehow moves into a person's spirit and that person begins his or her lifetime relationship with God. Thus, we can perceive His presence through our spirit. But when we are separated from Him, His voice is a distant and quiet tugging that can easily be drowned out by our noisy and busy lives. That distant and quiet tugging is what I had experienced all of my life.

In our family, we all believed in Jesus in a theoretical and historical sort of way, but we never really had a relationship with Him. It was like having a present and never opening it or using it. Imagine if someone bought you a blender, but you never opened the box or used it. In theory, you had a blender and you believed that it existed, but if you never used it, you would have never gotten the benefit of it.

It is so simple, yet we missed it. One by one, after Janet became a Christian, the rest of our family also became Christians. It seemed like the Holy Spirit was moving through our family to begin a much needed journey of healing for all of us. It was especially difficult for me because it meant admitting that I had not really been a Christian before. I finally put down my pride and asked Jesus to forgive me for all of my sins. I also asked Him to teach me how to live differently – how to depend on Him.

Becoming Christians gave all of us a sense of peace and well-being. We now had freedom from having to make all of the decisions on our own. We could ask God, who loved us and who knew all things to show us what to do. In my case, once I accepted Jesus as my Savior, it was as though a veil was removed from my face. I began to study the Bible more. Now that I was getting to know God in an intimate and personal way, I could look back on my life and see the events from God's different viewpoint.

AND then I realized that Jesus was the one who answered my prayer on Heinz's funeral. He was carrying me. I had been praying all night, truly out of complete desperation, because I knew that I no longer had the strength to pretend that I was fine. The peace that I experienced that morning was a direct answer to my prayer. In the Bible it says, *"Do not be anxious about anything, but in everything, by prayer and petition with thanksgiving present your requests to God. And the peace of God which transcends all understanding will guard your hearts and your minds in Christ Jesus." Philippians 4:6-7.* That is exactly what I experienced; there is no better way to describe it.

*****

"I am the Way, the Truth, and the Life; no man comes to the Father except through me." John 14:6

—18—

My Life Today

It has been more than 30 years since Heinz died. Many of my life's decisions had been based on fear and insecurity. It was one of the main reasons why I left Germany. I feared the governmental changes and I never wanted to experience wars and fanaticism again. It took a long time to change my behaviors. Praying and spending time with God had become so important. Over time, I became a lot less fearful, as I learned to trust that God would have everything under control.

I had been retired for almost 15 years when I realized it was time to sell the house that Heinz and I had bought at 9912 Medway Rd. I was 74 years old, and I had lived there for 46 years. I prayed about what to do for a long time, because it was a difficult decision, but I knew it was the right one. Janet, Carol, and Robert took turns on weekends to help me clean things out of the house. I appreciated their help—and I know I couldn't have done it without them. Still, it was very hard for me to get rid of old clothes, games, furniture, kitchen items, and books. Heinz and I had a set of encyclopedias that were very expensive when we bought the books in 1970, but by 2005, I could not even give them away.

The closing date for our home was scheduled for mid-June of 2006. Janet, Carol, Robert, and their families and I celebrated each last holiday at 9912 Medway Road with much joy, and some sadness, as we knew it would be the last time there.

That spring, the Lord gave me a very special and personal gift. Right outside the side door, on the railing, so that it was at about waist level, a robin had made a nest. The branches from an overgrown holly bush had enveloped the hand rail, and that is where this robin chose to place its nest. Each time I walked out of the house, I saw the nest, first with its four bright blue eggs, then the little hatchlings, and finally the little baby birds. I was so happy to see the mother robin feed her baby birds before I moved. The nest was empty by June, when the title to the home was transferred to the new owners. This is a memory I will treasure always as a sign of His love and care as I ventured into the next phase of my life.

After we sold the house, I moved to a retirement home in Hatboro, PA, a suburb just outside of Philadelphia, close to all my children. Just before I moved, one of my friends from our German Club asked me, "Well, how do you think Heinz would feel knowing that you sold the house?" I think this man was hoping to knock me down a bit. I replied, flatly, "Heinz has been dead for almost 30 years. I have been making all the decisions since then." Carol was with me when this conversation took place, and she told me my answer showed her how much I had changed over the years: I was annoyed and insulted, but I wasn't going to just say nothing; I let him know, in a controlled voice, that my decision was my decision, and it was really none of his business.

Today, I live on the second floor in a wonderful little apartment. My apartment has a small modern kitchen with dark blue countertops and blue-flowered wallpaper. There is a cut-out window in the wall from the kitchen that I can look through, into the living room, when I am working at the sink. My living room is large enough for my round maple kitchen table, my multi-colored sectional sofa, a recliner, my dark brown china cabinet, and my television. My bathroom has shower with handicap accessories. I have a small patio with a railing that just has enough space for two green plastic lawn chairs and a small table. From there, I have a nice view of a neighboring elementary school. Large maple and oak trees hug the school building.

My bedroom is one of my favorite places in my apartment. After 50 years, I finally replaced the grey bedroom set that I had had since I got married, which had been Heinz's before we married and which I never really liked. I bought a beautiful cherry set, complete with built-in photo frames for my grandchildren around the mirror on the dresser. I also treated myself to new bedroom curtains and matching bedding. It is a lovely room, and I enjoy looking at all the pictures of all my family. In fact, all of the walls in my apartment are crowded with pictures of my children's high-school and college graduations, their wedding pictures, and my grandchildren at various stages in their lives. There is no order to the way the pictures are placed on the wall. Some are hung high, some low. The frames are all different, some wooden, some gold, some silver, all various sizes. It doesn't matter to me whether they match or fit; I just want to have as many pictures of my family as possible. Janet married Bob Uetz in 1983, and they have two sons, John and Stephen, both of whom are married now. I have their high-school graduation pictures, their college graduation pictures, and now their wedding pictures. In 1988, Carol married Mike Thomson, and they have three children, Christina, Scott, and Ryan: I have Christina's and Scott's high-school graduation pictures, too. They are younger than Janet's children, and I hope there will be many more happy occasions in their lives that I can celebrate with pictures on my wall for many years to come. In 2003, Robert married Beth Bloss and I'm so happy to have their wedding picture as well. I know other people would say my apartment is full of "clutter," but I love all my pictures: I feel surrounded by my family.

*****

"How great is the love the Father has lavished on us, that we should be called children of God."

1John 3:1

—19—

A Last Visit with Renate

In 2005, Renate was diagnosed with Stage 4 ovarian cancer. Having recently heard of a young woman who died within a few months with Stage 4 ovarian cancer, I did not expect that Renate would have much time left. However, sometimes information can get lost in translation, so I did not want to be too pessimistic when we first heard the news about Renate. In a few weeks, she was identified as a candidate for a new type of chemotherapy that was being tried in Germany, and Renate was thrilled to have an opportunity to participate in this program.

To everyone's surprise, my sister had an amazing tolerance for the chemotherapy. Although her cancer remained, it moved into a period of remission while she was on the treatments. She was able to go through numerous repeated cycles of chemotherapy. Even though she lost her hair and was unusually tired from the treatment, she was able to get through the treatments and thoroughly enjoyed four more years to live her life to the fullest.

A special gift for Renate during this time was the birth of her great- granddaughter Josie. There seemed to be a special connection between the two of them, and they brought life and joy to each other. I often thought that watching Josie grow was keeping Renate going long beyond any time period that medical science would have predicted.

In 2008, Janet and her husband Bob were in the UK for six months because of Janet's job, and they took advantage of the proximity to the continent to visit our family in Germany one weekend. They stayed at my niece Marion's home and enjoyed three days with Renate, her daughter Marion, and my brother Karl Heinz and their families. Janet told me it was a wonderful time—especially because she got to see Renate. She told me my sister was full of life, humor, and joy.

When Bob and Janet returned from the UK, she suggested I think about visiting Germany again. I had been back to Germany many times after that first trip with Heinz in 1975. My Mama and Papa lived to be 93 and 88, respectively, and I enjoyed every moment I was privileged to share with them. When my Papa died, I went to Germany for his funeral, and my sisters and brothers gave me his zither: they knew how much I loved him and his talent. Today, I have it prominently displayed in my china cabinet. On another trip, I visited with Heinz's father, Paul, before he died at the age of 82. I wanted to tell him more of what happened to Heinz, but he immediately cut me off. "You do not have to tell me anything, Anita. Heinz was just unlucky. That is it. I do not want you to have to talk about it anymore," Paul said. I appreciated his sensitivity, and I was pleased to notice that he wore one of the shirts that had belonged to Heinz.

Even though I had seen my parents and Heinz's family five or six times since I retired, Janet thought I should go again and visit Renate while she was still doing so well, so we would really be able to enjoy each other's company. I had been thinking I could wait a year or two, but Janet had a sense of urgency that it would be best for me to go soon. Janet also mentioned that I had told her so many stories about my childhood growing up in Germany, but she had never been to those places with me, and she wanted to go with me. I sensed that she felt that the opportunities for her to visit those places with me might not be available too much longer, either, since my health and mobility had been gradually diminishing over the years. So she began persuading me that we should go together, and that we should do it in April of 2009 as a special trip for Janet's 50th birthday. Janet said it would be a wonderful way for her to celebrate this special birthday, but it also gave us a way of explaining the visit without having to say directly that we wanted to visit Renate one last time before she died.

So we told the family in Germany of our intentions, and Renate went into action organizing the time for us. She made sure there was ample time to spend with the family based in the Berlin area, including my brother Hans and his family and my other sister Erika, who lived in Prenzlau on the northern coast of Germany, but whose two daughters lived in Berlin. Renate also arranged time for us to enjoy my brother Karl-Heinz's family and of course, Renate, her daughter Marion, and their families in Chemnitz.

We started our trip in Berlin and spent several fun-filled days getting to know Hans and Erika's families. It was so wonderful for me to spend time with my sister and brother and tell stories from our childhood. Janet also enjoyed meeting her cousins, because they were all adults and they found they shared common interests, values, and even their sense of humor. She told me she couldn't believe she felt so at home with people she had only just met, yet there's something about a family bond that she hadn't experienced before because I did not have my sisters' and brothers' families near me, of course, when Janet, Carol, and Robert were growing up. We were an ocean away from each other.

When we arrived in Chemnitz, Renate and I were reunited, and I knew immediately that the trip was exactly the right thing to do at the right time. Even though it was over a year since Bob and Janet had visited, Renate was still full of life and able to enjoy our visit. However, there were signs that she was weakening due to the cancer. Janet said Renate was losing weight and seemed to be quite a bit thinner than the last time she had seen her. It also became clear, from that first day, that her energy was limited: she could spend only short periods of time with us, only two or three hours, and then she needed to rest. Nevertheless, Renate had planned our schedule of events with her usual flair for blending a good time with her practical and common sense nature not to overdo it. She made sure there was time for Janet to explore the area with me, since Janet wanted to hear me talk about my memories of Chemnitz, including visiting the spot where our home was destroyed by bombs and also visiting my elementary and high schools, which were still standing.

Renate even arranged a very special Easter Sunday for us. We attended the church where Renate and I had sung in the choir as little girls, and then we enjoyed a sumptuous meal at a restaurant overlooking the "Schlossteich," a little pond where my Mama used to take us to play when we were children.

On Janet's 50th birthday, the day started with a special breakfast with special decorations and a "happy birthday" song where the chorus repeated "how wonderful that you were born." Then we visited the Erzgebirge region, had a fabulous lunch at a local restaurant atop one of the mountains, climbed a lookout tower to see the full splendor of the mountain range, and shopped in a wonderful folk art store. Renate and her husband Roland, along with Marion and her husband Wolfgang, came with us. In the evening, Renate arranged for my Marion, Janet, and I to see *Fiddler on the Roof* in the Chemnitz opera house where my Papa used to play trumpet and where he often took me along for performances or rehearsals. I showed Janet where the orchestra pit was and where we used to sit as family of the orchestra. I was happy but also sad to relive those precious memories from my childhood, but it meant so much to me to be able to share this important part of my life with at least one of my children.

A few days later, Renate arranged for the whole family to come to visit for a picnic, and they sang special German songs for Janet with lyrics of love, appreciation, and recognition of the life of someone special. I could see that Janet was overwhelmed with the love of so many family members surrounding her; she told me later that she would never forget that very special gift of love from Renate.

For me, this trip was a bittersweet journey. While I loved sharing my childhood memories with Janet, I also wanted to cherish every minute I could with my sister. Renate made sure there was a day for her, Karl Heinz, and me to spend some private time together. That day was a treasure of love and honesty that I will carry with me forever. We talked about what was coming ahead for Renate and how much we would always be there for each other. We recalled some of the difficult times we had weathered together in the past and how we were mutually strengthened by knowing we were all in it together, no matter what came along or where we lived.

Renate and I shared a cup of coffee and conversation every day while Janet and I were there. We talked about the past; we talked about the present, about the wonderful experiences we were sharing together; and we talked about the future. We simply cherished every moment we had together.

After our visit, we learned that Renate's health began to decline more rapidly. She continued to feel weak and needed more and more rest. She was not tolerating the chemotherapy as much as she did in the past, and eventually, her doctors told her there was nothing more they could do for her. When Renate received that news, she understood and she recognized how much of a gift the past four years since her diagnosis had been.

In 2010, there were two important milestones that Renate hoped she would live to experience. Her granddaughter Katrin was pregnant with her second child, and Renate wanted to be able to meet this grandbaby. God was gracious and allowed her to meet little Joann and share in the joy of this new birth with the family. The second milestone was two months later, when Renate's other granddaughter Claudia would be graduating college as an architect and receiving the results of the architecture certification exam. Renate was also able to experience this joy with family as she learned of Claudia's success in passing the certification exam and receiving her diploma as a fully credentialed professional. Now she could go in peace, knowing that her family was well, that each of her granddaughters was established in life, and that there was much love and kindness in the family.

When the word came in May 2010 that Renate had taken her last breath, it was a sad day for all of us, but I was comforted somewhat by knowing that Renate lived to experience these important times with her grandchildren. I was also so grateful to have my memories and photos from my visit to Germany with Janet the year before, to remember my precious sister and the special bond that we shared, even though we were physically separated for most of our lives.

I also realized God's love and grace were with me in the timing of my visit with Renate. There was no more perfect time for us to spend together. Only six months after we returned home, I was diagnosed with congestive heart failure, and because I now need oxygen, it is unlikely I will ever be able to travel outside of the country again. And six months after that, Renate passed away. I have told Janet over and over how glad I am that she talked me into going when we did. It was a narrow window of opportunity not only for Renate but for me as well. I was still able to travel, and Renate still felt well enough to truly enjoy the visit.

I cried many tears the day I learned Renate was gone – tears of grief, tears of sympathy for those Renate left behind, tears of gratitude that God allowed Renate to live to be part of her family's important milestones, and tears of awe at the feet of a God who knows the end from the beginning and who graciously and mercifully directs our steps to show us His great love and tender care over each and every detail in our lives.

Sometimes, we can think that God is so big that the small details of our lives can't possibly be a concern to Him. Yet I look back on my last trip and those precious days and know that God Himself orchestrated them as a gift to us and as a gift to Renate.

*****

"For this is what the high and lofty One says—he who lives forever, whose name is holy: I live in a high and holy place, but also with him who is contrite and lowly in spirit, to revive the spirit of the lowly and to revive the heart of the contrite."

Isaiah 57:15

—20—

Reflections on My Life

All my life, I was looking for God. I sang in church choirs, and I wanted to do the right things. I was excited on my confirmation day and very serious about it, too. But I felt empty somehow; I knew that if God was really there, there had to be more to the Christian life than what I was experiencing. When I encountered Helmut's mother in West Germany, I was taken aback by her faith and simple trust in the Lord. She seemed to have some connection with God that was foreign to me. Realizing that I was searching, she often prayed with me and offered to study the Bible with me. In her own way, she was trying to show me that the Bible held the answers I needed for my life. After all these years, I still have that Bible and that worn out folded piece of paper where she wrote down, in pencil, a few suggested Bible verses for me to read. When I think over them now, I realize she was trying to teach me to trust the Lord and not my own strength and abilities.

The churches I went to in Germany and the Feltonville Lutheran Church in Philadelphia were good churches and the gospel was preached there. Like many other people who go to church, I just never really perceived and grasped the message. Physically going to church is not enough.

As I got to know Janet's husband, Bob, it was evident to me how he really trusted the Lord with everything in his life. I knew that I wanted to be able to trust the Lord with everything in my life, too. He helped explain the simple message of salvation to me. It started with recognizing that I was a sinner, which was not so easy for a proud German like me. I became aware that sin was blocking my access to God. The Bible makes clear that Jesus' death on the cross was for my personal sin and that He rose again. I received His forgiveness and began a relationship with God. I just needed to ask. Now I have a relationship with the Lord that gives me peace, hope, contentment, and the assurance of heaven. I can talk to the Lord about anything and everything in my life. He doesn't always answer me immediately, but I sense that He has everything under control and that He will lead me in the way that is best.

Trusting the Lord does not mean that there will not be any valleys. In those valleys, often a deeper and more intimate relationship with God is formed.

We all will have regrets. I wish I could have been stronger for my children. I did not stand up enough for the children, with Heinz. I always felt sorry for Heinz and saw his insecurities. With Jesus' gentle coaxing in my spirit and with the strength He supplied, I had to forgive Heinz and I had to receive His forgiveness for myself. That is so freeing. I am forgiven and can leave the past behind.

Looking back at the journey through my life, so many experiences rush back into my memory. Whether in good times or in frightening times, I can now see more clearly how the Lord was guiding and leading until I finally accepted Him.

I am so thankful that He guided me through the horrors of Hitler's Third Reich. He gave me a loving family that remembered we were children and tried to find joy amidst the horror of war. He was there when my sister Renate and I needed his protection, when both of us lay in a ditch on a lonely country road, while war planes unloaded their ammunition above us just weeks before this terrible war ended. Not one piece of shrapnel came near us. It was as if His hand was covering us and shielding us from the onslaught. This protection did not come because we were better than anyone else or because we deserved it somehow. It was in His plan to protect us on that day, so we might tell of His love.

He was with my family and me as we somehow managed to endure the years after the war, when food was scarce and Communism controlled East Germany. Somehow, we always found food and miraculously remained healthy through that time. Although I didn't recognize it, God gave me the courage to flee to America, to what I hoped would be a free world. He blessed me with a sister who possessed more strength than I had, at a time when I was paralyzed with fear, as I attempted to go to Berlin and try to find my way to freedom. Our former neighbor, Frau Herta Fischer, and her sister-in-law, Frau Hildegard Schiller, were also undoubtedly gifts from God. How else can one explain the generosity of this person, to lend money to someone she didn't even know, for a plane ticket as well as for railroad expenses? This was not all that long after the war, and no one had any extra money.

The nuns at the hospital in West Germany were also placed in my path to teach me how to live out their faith by showing mercy in the name of Jesus to all who came across their path.

When I got to this country, He continued to provide for me. It was absolutely no accident that Paula and I met and became life-long friends. The job I found was, of all places, in a Jewish owned sweater mill—and I was a recent immigrant from Germany and couldn't even sew! God's handprints were all over that situation. All these years we have known each other, Paula has been like a sister and my friend. We have shared our good times as well as difficult times. Paula was there with me when Heinz was in the hospital, she was with us at his bedside after he died, and she comes with me to visit his grave a few times a year. Even after I could no longer bend down to take care of his gravesite, Paula tends it for me: she plants new flowers, pulls out the weeds, and does whatever else is needed. She has been my best friend through all these years.

The overwhelming sense of peace that I experienced the day of Heinz's funeral was a direct answer to my desperate pleas to God for help. I was afraid of completely falling apart that day. I had been through so much already and I just did not feel like I could go on. I was despairing of life. The experience of God's presence on that day is something that I am incapable of justly describing. I believe that Heinz's last words to me, about finally being able to pray, meant that he had accepted God's love through His son Jesus. I don't know why he had to suffer so much, why he had to be in such excruciating pain from his burned body for fourteen days. We do not know the answer to that, but God allowed it to happen. Perhaps it was the only way to get the attention of this depressed and hardened man, so that he would be able to find God before he died. I didn't realize this until many years later, when I embraced God in my own life, but I believe that's what happened to Heinz then. I also believe that one day I will see him again in Heaven.

Thinking back over Heinz's last year and half of his life also shows me how God was guiding and leading. We never had any extra money, and yet Heinz was suddenly determined to go back to Germany to see our parents again, because as he put it, "they were getting older and we may never see them again". On that same trip we completely retraced his steps from East Germany to West Germany and to America. Heinz was able to thank many of the people who had helped him along the way. And then there were the very generous Christmas presents for each of our children that he purchased himself. He had never done that before—I had always bought everything. When we were first married Heinz had bought some personal gifts (like jewelry) for me, but it had been a long time since he had bought anything very personal for me. Even when he did buy a gift, it was usually immediately before the event. And yet, about a month before our 20th anniversary, Heinz had bought that beautiful watch to give to me. As it turns out, he was in the hospital on our actual anniversary day. My only explanation for Heinz's behavior was that God guided him to do these things, even though Heinz was unaware of it.

I'm so grateful that the Lord put people in my life at just the perfect time. Today, some of my friends belong to the German Club whose members came from the same area of Germany that I did many years ago. We—Lina, Lore, Erika (who has recently passed), and Margaret and I—celebrate our birthdays and special events. Of course, we do our best to never miss a choir rehearsal as we share our fondness for singing and music. My friend Lina is also a great cook, and it's always a pleasure to be in her company. Lore has gone on several trips with me: together, we explored the beauty of the places God created for us to enjoy. Horst, Elfriede, Günter, John (who recently passed away), Theresa, and Ann have also been my friends for many years. I'm so grateful that Jesus placed these people in my life, so we can be supportive of each other.

From the window of my apartment at the retirement facility I now reside in, I can see a middle school. A few of the talented teachers there decided to offer a writing course for senior citizens—which is part of what led to my desire to write this book. It's such a privilege to be part of this venture. Thank you, Lord. During one of these classes, the teacher asked us to write a letter to our grandchildren, and this is what I wrote:

My dear grandchildren, John, Stephen, Christina, Scott, and Ryan,

The door into my eighties is slightly ajar. No one knows how long one's life will last, so when you reach this milestone, you feel compelled to talk about life.

As a young person, you think you have all the answers. You soon find out that your existence is a lifelong learning experience. You'll all make your own mistakes. Learn from them. Remember your family is the single most constant in your life. No one is perfect; however, you know your family will always be there for you. They tell you the truth even if you don't want to hear it. They teach you, love you, and will be there for you always. When your entire family lives in Germany, as in my situation, you know how important family truly is.

Your parents taught you about the Lord. However, you have to find your own personal relationship. There will always be questions. Sometimes, you find an answer, and other times, you don't. It's not easy to understand what the Lord is conveying to you. It takes a long time until you reach true understanding. You strip yourself of everything, and events in your life become so clear. You can finally see the Lord's walk in your life. Then and only then, you reach a grasp of understanding of the price Jesus paid so you can be his child.

Now let's talk about love. You all long for it, and when you think you've found it, make sure that love is not just a word. Love is the ultimate of human commitment. Love should be unselfish, supportive, giving, and forgiving. Listen with your heart not just your ears.

As you grow into adulthood, there are many highs and valleys. Disappointment will come your way as well as happy events. Love your life, embrace it. Share it with people you care about. Be a little forgiving of yourself: after all, you're only human. Treat others as you would want to be treated. Be a good friend to someone. Never settle, always look up. Discover something new, reach for the stars. Experience heart-pounding possibilities. Try something unfamiliar. Let music and the arts enrich your spirit. Love your life. Go for it!"

*****

Now, at age 79, I know that with Jesus' help, my three children grew up to be the joy of my life. God blessed each of my children with exactly the right life partner to share their lives. My four grandsons and my granddaughter, who I call "Princess," are such a gift from God, and I'm so thankful that the Lord gave me this life to live. Perhaps I had to experience the deep valleys I traveled through.

However, in His love for me, Jesus set me free from my insecurities and fear.

He took my hands and led me with His perfect love.

"So nimm den meine Haende und fuehre Mich, bis an mein selig Ende und ewiglich. Ich mag allein nicht gehen, nicht einen Schritt, wo Du wirst gehen und stehen, da nimm mich mit."

It means, "So take my hands and lead me until my blessed ending and until eternity. I do not want to go alone, not even one step. Take me with you, whether you go, or stop."

*****

"So do not fear, for I am with you; do not be dismayed, for I am your God. I will strengthen you and help you. I will uphold you with my righteous right hand." Isaiah 41:10

—21—

Closure

Thanksgiving... Things I am grateful and thankful for:

The special time with family and friends

The distinctive aroma only a turkey roasting in the oven could produce

The special pies my family bakes

The games we play after dinner

The special walk through rustling leaves

The brisk air kissing my cheeks

The laughs of my grandchildren

The warm and cozy feeling of a fireplace

My first grandchild who was born on a thanksgiving day

The love of the Lord for giving me this life.

—Anita Plutte

This is the Bornholmerbruecke, the bridge that connected the Russian zone in East Berlin to the French zone in West Berlin. During my 1996 trip to Germany, I retraced my steps across this bridge that I had crossed so anxiously years earlier, when Renate helped me leave East Germany through Berlin, and so many dear people helped me come to the United States afterwards.

During my 1981 trip to Germany, my Papa played the zither for me: He was so talented on so many musical instruments. I am so happy to have his zither today to remind me of him playing it. The large "pyramide", in the background on the left, is one he made himself.

During 1992, I returned to Germany for my Papa's funeral. This photo was taken a restaurant in Frohburg following the funeral: Me, Renate, Hans, Mama, Karl-Heinz and Erika.

Mama and me, in Renate's flower garden in 1998. My Mama lived to be 93, but this was the last time I saw her. I made the trip that year to celebrate her 90th birthday.

Over the years I was blessed to have so many friends, many of whom came to celebrate my 70th birthday (in 2002): Lina, Elfriede, Lore, Margaret, Ann, Paula (standing) and Ann, me, Erika (seated), with Irmgard kneeling in front of us.

Before going to the church on Janet's wedding day, June 25, 1983: Robert, Janet, me, and Carol.

Carol's wedding day, June 18, 1988: Janet's husband, Bob, Carol and Mike and Robert (standing) with Janet holding son, John, and me (seated).

Robert's wedding day, November 15, 2003: Carol's son, Ryan, daughter, Christina, Mike, Carol's son, Scott, and Carol then me, Janet, Bob, and their sons, Stephen and John, with bride and groom, Beth and Robert, beaming in front.

Paula and me: We have been friends since 1957. This picture was taken on my 78th birthday in 2010 making us friends for 53 years at that point.

Janet's son, John's, wedding to Shanti Kulkarni in May, 2010: left to right, this is Bob's sister, Roberta, Roberta's daughter-in-law, Terri, with her daughter, Ashley, and her son, Anthony, who was the ring bearer; Roberta's son and Terri's husband, Michael, Beth and my son, Robert, the beautiful bride, Shanti, and John, me, with Bob behind me and Janet next to me; Carol's son Scott (wearing sunglasses), Janet's son, Stephen, Carol's son, Ryan, behind her daughter, Christina, and Mike behind Carol.

Janet's son, Stephen's, wedding to Sarah Yoder in July 2011: Back Row: Mike Thomson (Carol's husband) and Bob Uetz (Janet's husband); Left to Right, Beth & Rob Plutte, Shanti & John Uetz, Ryan and Scott Thomson (Carol's sons behind the bride and groom, the Bride and Groom, Sarah and Steve, Janet, me, Christina (Carol's daughter) and Carol.

Epilogue

—by Carol Thomson

A few days after Thanksgiving of 2009, our mother was hospitalized. At 78 years old, she was diagnosed with congestive heart failure at a local hospital, just outside of Philadelphia. We went to see her—Janet and her husband Bob, myself, and Robert—and we weren't happy to see her tethered to an oxygen machine, with a mask over her face. We had been talking about writing her memoirs for years, and when we realized she would be confined to her apartment a lot more, we decided to move forward with the book. It would take her mind off of her health problems, and it would be a great time for us to be together.

One by one as Janet, Robert, and I unpacked the sad memories that our mother had placed in that tightly closed drawer, we were forced to process them all over again, and it was very emotional for us. Even our mother was finally able to look on her life with perspective and grace; amazed again at how gracious God had been through all of it, especially the things she would have rather kept buried. It is very healing to let these experiences take their proper place in life as we look, remember, grieve, and forgive.

And yet, although Janet, Robert, and I became Christians after our father died, his behavior still had its effects on each of us:

Robert was reluctant to embrace the full responsibilities of adult life as a teenager. Because of insecurity, he was stifled as a young man and clung to his job at McDonald's for a long time. It was the path of least resistance, it kept him busy, he earned a good salary, and it taught him valuable life lessons, yet he had so many more gifts that were lying dormant in this lifestyle. He stayed there as a manager for twelve years before deciding to go to college in his late 20s. After a five- year program, he became an architect.

While he was growing in his architectural career, he was also growing and maturing in his faith in Christ. Gradually, he became more confident and began to participate in various ministries at church, both for his own growth and also to invest his life into the lives of others. It was through his work with the junior-high youth that he met his future wife, Beth. They were both in their 40s when they married, but God had a very special purpose in bringing them together when He did. Today, he and his wife Beth are planning to become missionaries among immigrants in the UK.

I finished college, became a CPA, and also received my MBA in finance. Lydia's parents generously paid for my graduate education. I married a godly man and we have three wonderful children. Mike and I are both involved in ministries at our church. But through all those years, I never learned how to completely relax and enjoy everyday life. I kept up that pace for over 45 years before I finally realized that I needed a break and had to slow down. The healing process takes time, but it is on God's schedule.

Janet graduated from college with a degree in biochemistry and later earned an M.S. in regulatory affairs, and she has worked at Johnson & Johnson for almost 30 years. Janet married a strong Christian man and they have two sons who are now married as well. Both Janet and Bob are also involved in church ministry. But she began to suffer from depression and panic attacks in her early 20s. Janet, too, needed to heal, and through her healing, she learned to lean on the Lord for everything. Both Janet and I needed to forgive our dad, and we have.

*****

Our mother looks at every day as a gift. As each year passes, she realizes she will be able to do less and less. She has a lot of trouble walking and needs her cane. Now with her dependence on the oxygen, she is somewhat more limited. But she is determined to make the most of each moment, day, or event. We all enjoy hanging out with our mom. And she loves being with us, and she really loves her five grandchildren. We cherish the time we have with her, and we are comforted knowing that she will be with Jesus when He calls her home.

Last, I would just like to say that it was difficult for our mother to admit to some of the terrible circumstances that took place while we were children. Many of her friends will have had no idea until they read this book. Her own strength, will, and positive personality served her well for a long time. **But eventually every person should realize that we were created to depend on and trust in a living God.** This is her message.

She also hopes to impress on the reader the importance of family and the importance of loving one's children just for who they are.

Her wishes are that a portion of the royalties from this book be directed to sharing the Gospel in Germany and that an equal portion of the royalties be directed to missions that bless Israel in the name of Jesus Christ, according to Genesis 12:3.

*****

"But those who hope in the Lord will renew their strength. They will soar on wings like eagles; they will run and not grow weary, they will walk and not be faint." Isaiah 40:31

Acknowledgments

I would like to thank my three children and five grandchildren for filling my life with love. I am also so thankful for my entire extended family in Germany. I would like to thank all of my friends in Germany and in America for enriching my life. And I would like to thank the Lord for saving me.

I also thank my daughters, Janet Uetz and Carol Thomson for helping me write these memoirs, my son Robert Plutte for designing the book cover and for reading and commenting on the manuscript. We would also like to thank Ruth Mills Walters (of Ruth Mills Literary Services, LLC) for her encouragement, enthusiasm, coaching, and invaluable assistance with this book. We also thank John Uetz, Christina Thomson, Joy Sarcewicz and Elizabeth Fraley-Hogg for reading versions of the manuscript, for their ideas, and for being bold enough to tell us why things needed to be written differently.

Also a special thanks to my sister Erika, who will use her talents to translate this book into the German language.

Appendix

The Adventures of Fuzzytail

For my grandchildren

*****

FUZZYTAIL'S EASTER SURPRISE

"It's almost Easter," shouted the little bunny children with joy.

"Now, now, children, settle down. We have so much to do before we can fill the Easter baskets," Bunny Dad said with hidden laughter in his voice. The bunny cave was buzzing with happy sounds and excitement.

Little Fuzzytail, the smallest one of the bunnies, rubbed his little eyes in wonder as he gazed upon the colorful Easter eggs, candy, and chocolate bunnies. Everything smelled so good. He was so excited and eager to help, but he tripped over the red paint which his brother, Rifflenose, used to make beautiful, colored eggs. "Go away!" his brother hollered. Sister Wiggletoe, didn't let him help either. He was too little and clumsy to pour the hot, melted chocolates into funny looking shapes to make yummy tasting chocolate bunnies and chickies. A great big tear rolled down his little, fuzzy cheeks and he sadly hopped into the kitchen to his bunny mommy.

"Why are you so sad?" she asked. "Ohhh, I am so little and too clumsy to help," he sobbed as he put his head in his mother's lap. "Let's see now, Fuzzytail, maybe you can help me do something," she said. Bunny Mommy found the tiniest little paintbrush and gave it to him. "Here are some candy eggs. They are still warm because I just made them, but they need some color. Perhaps you could make them look happy", she said. Fuzzytail dipped the teenie-weenie brush into the paint and put the most colorful little dots on the eggs. Each egg looked like a masterpiece.

After awhile, Bunny Mommy checked to see how Fuzzytail was doing. To her wonder, those plain looking candy eggs had the most colorful dots sprinkled all over them. "They are beautiful!!!" she exclaimed. "I know the children will love to find these eggs in their Easter baskets."

Finally, Easter morning arrived and all the baskets were hidden in the shrubs and behind the trees for the children to find. The bunnies watched from a distance when John and Stephen came running into the backyard to look for their Easter surprises. "John! I found my Easter basket", said Stephen. "It was hidden under the apple tree."

"Look at these great looking eggs" Johnny said, when he spotted his basket right next to the red and yellow tulips. Just down the street, their cousins, Christina, Scott, and Ryan were also looking for their baskets. Christina and Scott found three baskets hidden behind the swingset. They gave one to their brother, Ryan, who was still a baby and hadn't learned how to walk yet. Little Fuzzytail leaped for joy as he watched the children. They especially loved the eggs that he had made. "Look, Mom, everybody really likes the eggs I decorated!"

The entire bunny family watched as John, Stephen, Christina, Scott, and Ryan went with their parents to church as they went to celebrate the true joy of Easter. JESUS IS RISEN!

*****

FUZZYTAIL GOES TO SCHOOL

In September, children everywhere are getting ready to start the new school year. Mom bought new clothes for John. He is going into first grade. John asks his mother all about the big, yellow school bus while his brother, Stephen, asks if he could wear a cool shirt just like John. Everybody is happy and excited because today is the first day of school and Mom promised a special treat for John, Stephen, and their cousins Christina, Scott and Ryan when the school day ends.

Near the blueberry bushes in John and Stephen's yard lives the bunny family. Little Fuzzytail, the youngest one of the family, will also go to school for the first time. On his way to his schoolhouse, which is located at the bottom of the huge oak tree, he sees the yellow school bus go by. All of the children wave to their parents. Fuzzytail is a little bit nervous because his schoolhouse looks a little too big and scary. However, he is very curious and he enters the school.

His teacher is Miss Jellybean. She's already waiting for Fuzzytail and she shows him where his seat is in the classroom. "Now, now, children, quiet down", she says as she hands everybody a piece of paper and thick crayon. She asks the bunnies to draw a picture of something that they enjoyed doing during the summer. "Later you can tell us all about yourself", she said.

Little Fuzzytail didn't know where to begin. He had so much fun playing with his friends, brothers and sisters during the summer. They played ball, rode their bikes, went swimming and tasted luscious strawberries from the garden. Fuzzytail was a little frightened because he didn't know how to draw. Most of the bunny children had their drawings finished very quickly but Fuzzytail's paper was still blank. He was terrified and wished that he was safe at home with his mother. In desperation, he searched in his pants for something that he might be able to use. A piece of his carrot from his morning breakfast was exactly what he needed. He drew two circles on the paper using the carrot. He also found a little string that he used to connect the circles with. It represented the frame of his bike that he loves to ride.

One by one the other bunny children told their story to the class using their drawings. One little bunny drew one, big circle and told the class that this was the pond behind her house. Her entire family played there all summer long. Fuzzytail's friend, Tumblefoot, showed a picture of lettuce and spinach. Everybody laughed when he told them that he played hide & seek in Mr. Raindrop's vegetable garden. Fuzzytail was very happy because Miss Jellybean liked his picture a lot. She thought that bicycle riding must be a lot of fun.

The next morning, he was very eager to return to school where he was going to learn from Miss Jellybean how he could be the best bunny in the whole, wide world.

*****

FUZZYTAIL'S WINTER SURPRISE

BRRR, it's so cold outside. Snow is falling softly to the ground covering bushes, trees, rooftops and streets with its glittering, white blanket. Fuzzytail, who lives with his mom, dad, sister, and brothers in John and Stephen's backyard always had to check out the world around him. He runs into the yard! Soon his little, fuzzy cheeks are covered in snowflakes. Some of the snowflakes tumbled right into his wide, open mouth. He loved the taste. It reminds him of fresh spring water. His bunny sister and brothers are still sleeping in their warm beds. "Wake up, you sleepy heads!" He says with a voice full of excitement, "Let's go out and play in the snow!"

Meanwhile, a lot of activity is going on in John and Stephen's house. Their cousins, Christina, Scott, and Ryan, came for a visit. "Let's make a snowman," John suggested. First, Ryan plopped himself into the fresh, fallen snow to make a snow angel. At the end of the yard, where the bunnies lived, Fuzzytail and his siblings tried to do the same. However, it doesn't work because little bunnies can't flap their arms. Before long a snowball like figure stands proudly in the yard. The children worked hard to roll big snowballs and stack them on top of each other. "We need a hat and a face for our snowman," Scott says. Christina found small pebbles and the carrots and used them to create a beautiful face and nose that was just perfect. Stephen located the leftover buckets from the sandbox. The bucket turned into a perfect hat for the snowman. He's a sight to behold.

Mom brought the children into the house for some hot chocolate, with sweet toasted marshmallows on top. She gives each child a few Christmas cookies. They are so fresh and still a little warm and taste like vanilla, chocolate, and strawberries.

The next day is Christmas. The little room is graced with a decorated Christmas tree. Fire from the fireplace envelops the whole room with cozy, magical comfort. The aroma of the pine tree, baked apples, and sweet nuts completes the warm feeling of Christmas.

"Tomorrow we will all celebrate the birthday of Jesus", Dad says. "We received the greatest gift from Jesus, therefore we give each other special gifts on Christmas to remember his birthday," Mom explained. "We children should give something to the animals that live in our backyard," John suggests. What an exciting thought! "Let's make a Christmas surprise for the bunnies and the birds!!!" Everyone shouted at once. Soon the birdhouse is filled with colorful birdseed. A wicker basket full of cut up carrots and apple peels is a treat for the bunny family.

The next day, after church, the children and their families peek into the backyard. The bunny family is still enjoying the delicious carrots and apple peels. Many hungry birds flutter around the bird-feeder and on the ground below. The children made a promise to themselves to take care of the needs of animals who give them so much joy all year long.

(Endnotes)

[1] Santa Claus

[2] Written by Julie von Hausmann in 1862

[3] Dorla was actually Heinz's aunt who was helping us facilitate all of these arrangements – we had to be secretive in our letters and be very careful not to implicate anyone since much of what we were doing would be considered illegal in East Germany. We also assumed that our mail to East Germany was being intercepted and read, so we didn't want to take chances that would impact someone else in any of our letters.

[4] The story of Fuzzytail is included in the appendix at the end of the book.

CPSIA information can be obtained at www.ICGtesting.com
Printed in the USA
BVOW070935211211

278832BV00002B/5/P

9 781619 044098